BEYOND SUSPICION

BEYOND SUSPICION

RUSSELL WILLIAMS: A CANADIAN SERIAL KILLER

ALAN R. WARREN

COPYRIGHT

BEYOND SUSPICION: Russell Williams: A Canadian Serial Killer
Written by Alan R. Warren

Published in Canada

Copyright @ 2020 by Alan R. Warren

All rights reserved. No part of this book may be reproduced, scanned, or distributed in any printed or electronic form without permission of the author. The unauthorized reproduction of a copyrighted work is illegal. Criminal copyright infringement, including infringement without monetary gain, is investigated by the FBI and is punishable by fines and federal imprisonment. Please do not participate in or encourage privacy of copyrighted materials in violation of the author's rights. Purchase only authorized editions.

This is a work of nonfiction. No names have been changed, no characters invented, no events fabricated.

Cover design, formatting, layout, and editing by Evening Sky Publishing Services

CONTENTS

Preface vii
Introduction ix

1. To Be Young Again — 1
2. Welcome To Our Town — 11
3. Mistaken Identity — 27
4. Murder Of Corporal Marie-France Comeau — 43
5. Murder Of Jessica Lloyd — 51
6. Won't You Be My Neighbor — 59
7. Objects May Appear Closer Than They Are — 73
8. Interrogation Of Russell Williams — 77
9. Confessions Of A Madman — 121
10. Is That What I Think It Is? — 175
11. Trial Of Russell Williams — 187
12. Who Are The People In Your Neighborhood? — 193
13. When All Is Said, And Done — 203
    Epilogue — 209

Acknowledgments 211
About the Author 213
Also By Alan R. Warren 215
References And Sources 219

PREFACE

"In the beginning, it was all black and white." – Maureen O'Hara

His mind worked very efficiently, remembering all the details right down to the subtlest of changes that would happen. When he was on his daily jog through the neighborhood, he would always have a smile for everyone he met. He would stop to help ladies trying to carry their groceries into their house, or help retrieve a runaway ball for kids playing hockey in the street.

Yes, he was the type of man that we all wanted in our neighborhoods; not only was he pleasant and very helpful, but he was an officer who served our country in wars, put his life on the line for our freedom and way of life.

Everyone who lived around him looked forward to seeing him on his jog, wave, smile, maybe even talk a little about things going on around us or in the world. So, when the news came out about him being a serial killer, rapist, and the man who broke into people's homes and stole personal garments, you could only imagine the deep sudden shock people felt.

This is the true story of Russell Williams. Once the model of a military man, now he sits convicted of a series of crimes that include two counts of first-degree murder, brutal sexual assaults, and 82 home invasions that included a series of strange thefts.

Colonel Russell Williams once seemed the embodiment of the military ideals of duty and honor: a pilot for the Prime Minister and Queen Elizabeth of England, commander of the secret Canadian Air Force Base in the Persian Gulf, and in 2009 appointed commanding officer of Canada's largest, most important Air Force Base in Trenton, Ontario.

Russell Williams's fall from grace is a frightening reminder of the unpredictability of human behavior.

INTRODUCTION

It was just after dusk when Russell Williams left his cabin for his nightly jog. It was mid fall, and it looked like winter was settling into the area a little early this year. The weather was its usual damp, dark and wet November, but slightly chilled through the air, so he had an extra layer of clothes on to keep him warm, as he would be out a little longer than usual tonight.

Williams had selected a route which he had taken three times before this night, so he was somewhat familiar with the roads he planned on taking and knew the distance and time he would need. So why would he be out longer tonight?

Williams was not only running to keep in shape, but he also wanted to do some investigating while he was out. What kinds of things do you investigate on a jog, you might ask? There was a certain house he was keeping an eye on and wanted to make sure he knew all the comings and goings of. Was Williams being a good man and watching a house of one of his neighbors while they were out of town on a vacation?

Not exactly.

Well, yes, he was keeping an eye on his neighbor's house, but they were not away on vacation. In fact, they were living out their average daily routines, like the kids going to school, the father and mother both going to their jobs, getting groceries, and collecting the mail. Nothing out of the ordinary going on there.

So why the interest? Why is the Colonel watching his neighbor's house? If he's not keeping an eye on their property while they're away, why would a high-ranking officer in the armed forces be so curious about his neighbors that he actually routed his daily jog by their home?

Perhaps they were some sort of threat to the country? Maybe they had terrorist ties to the family? This makes for a very curious situation.

On this fourth planned run by the home of the Colonel's neighbors, he stopped just as he arrived in front of their house. Williams bent down and began to what looked like tie his shoe, something that happens to me all the time. It seems like my laces are always too long, and they come untied several times during a run or even a walk.

Only, it seemed to be taking quite a long time for him to tie his shoes. I wonder what's wrong? Did his shoelace break? He now started to stand. He took a sharp left and ran into the dark shadows of the street and behind the house. What was he doing?

Williams was now crouched down among three large shrubs that were planted just beside the sidewalk that led to the basement of the house. After a solid five minutes passed, he crept down the stairway and leaned against the basement door. He then seemed to be listening for any sounds, his head pressed against the door. Williams then pressed the right side of his body against the door while his hands were fiddling with the door knob, and suddenly it opened.

He slipped into the basement and closed the door in a split second.

1

TO BE YOUNG AGAIN

"It takes a long time to become young." - Pablo Picasso

David Russell Williams was born in Bromsgrove, Worcestershire, England on March 7, 1963, to Christine Nonie (nee Chivers) and Cedric David Williams. His father received his PhD in metallurgy (a material scientist who specializes in metals) and was from a privileged family, the son of a British civil defense officer. His mother was from a well-to-do family in which her father was an executive with British Petroleum Oil.

His family immigrated to Canada and they moved to Chalk River, Ontario where his father was hired as a metallurgist at Canada's premiere nuclear research facility, Chalk River Laboratories. It was once a top-secret installation created to help the United States with the Manhattan Project, a research and development project during World War II that produced the first nuclear weapons.

This was a great place to raise two boys as well, being only a short distance from Camp Petawawa, where they would be entranced with the constant military flyovers. This was probably where Russell would have caught the flying bug, looking up at the incredible aircraft that would fly over.

After relocating to Chalk River, the Williams family met another family, the Sovkas, Jerry and Marilynn, who moved only about one block away from them. Both being new to town, they soon they became close friends. Jerry was a nuclear physicist from Alberta and the son of Czechoslovakian immigrants. Marilynn was born in Glasgow, Scotland and was the daughter of a doctor. The two families would end up spending a lot of time together. They would hire one babysitter who would take care of both families' children in one of their homes while the parents spent time together in the other home.

The town was considered quite a conservative town, but there was a small group of people who were involved in a "swingers club" where they would be involved in swapping out each other's wives. We do not know if the Williams and Sovkas were involved in this group, but it comes into question later when they ended up divorcing and remarrying each others spouses.

It was not long after they were settled in their new life that Christine, Russell's mother, opened her own private physiotherapy practice, specializing in children's needs. This was not a popular thing to do in the community, as in those days it was not thought of too well that a wife of a prominent PhD would work outside of her home; a good wife would stay at home with the family. This business would also be considered a challenge to her husband as the breadwinner of the family.

Perhaps this was the start of the drifting apart in their relationship. By the time Russell turned six, his mother had packed up the two boys and moved to their own residence. The breakup was smooth at the beginning, with both parents settling on a visitation schedule and finances. But soon after that it took a turn for the worse, as Christine found out that David was having an affair with Marilynn Sovka. This was a painful betrayal, as Marilynn had been such a close friend to Christine. The rumors spread in the small town quickly, as there weren't many places to hide such a thing. Christine filed for divorce soon afterwards.

This divorce was the reason for an evaluation on Russell, the first that we have on record. The following is a copy of the report:

"David Russell, born on March 7, 1963, in Bromsgrove, England, is in good health and appears to be an active, precious child with an interest in life and people. He appears to have a close relationship with the petitioner (mother), who is very involved in her children's activities. Russell appears very compatible with his brother. He is attending grade one in the Herman Street Public School, Petawawa, and appears above average in reading and printing ability. His

> creative ability appears mature and vocabulary expansive. Russell's relationship with the respondent (father) is also very close, and he enjoys visits with him."

Exactly one week after the Williamses dissolved their marriage, the Sovkas had officially ended their marriage as well. Now, while all of this was happening, the former Mrs. Williams and Mr. Sovka had somehow fallen in love, and not only ended up moving in with each other, they were married only four months later. It was such a scandal in the community that they felt forced to move away, and they moved to North York, a suburb of Toronto. This way they could start fresh where nobody would know of their past. This was also when Russell and his brother took their new stepfather's last name and became Sovkas.

Meanwhile, his father David tried staying in town with Marilynn as his new girlfriend, but they only lasted a year before they felt compelled to move as well. They found the tension mounting and thought moving away would relieve that, so they headed to New York, but that didn't help, and they found themselves separating within a year of their move.

Russell then began high school at Toronto's Birchmount Park Collegiate and started to deliver the *Globe and Mail* newspaper for work. His mother had him taking piano lessons, and he joined the school band where he played the trumpet. It was there that Russell met his first girlfriend, Sara, who was a flute player in the school band. Sara was known as a happy girl who liked to play jokes on others.

They were inseparable for the two years that they dated. Nobody knows the reasons they broke up or how Russell handled it.

By 1979, Russell's family was on the move again. This time they moved to South Korea where Jerry, his stepfather, was to oversee another reactor project. Neither of the boys seemed to settle very well in their new home or with the new culture. In fact, Russell was apparently disturbed by the way that women were treated in South Korea. He would find himself getting into fights with the Korean men, as they liked to spit on the women that they were angry with.

| High School Photo

After only one year, Russell was sent back to Toronto, and he completed his final two years of high school as a boarding student at Toronto's Upper Canada College while his parents stayed in South Korea.

One of his roommates at college ended up becoming a lifelong friend, Jeff Farquhar. Russell was known as a real prankster among the dorm. "He would do things like put plastic wrap over their toilet bowls, or pour soy sauce in somebody's unattended drink." Jeff claimed. "He seemed to have a passion for catching his roommates off guard, hiding in the closet and jumping out to scare them."

Soon, the life of every woman on campus was about to change in a much more terrifying way than any of the pranks Russell liked to play on any of them. In May of 1987, a series of brutal attacks and rapes began on campus, and the perpetrator was soon to become known as the "Scarborough Rapist." In many of the cases reported, women were followed getting off their school bus and assaulted quite viciously in nearby parks or parking lots.

Several years, later Paul Bernardo was linked by DNA to many of the rapes that were committed during the years of 1987-1990. Bernardo has since been convicted and now serves life in Kingston Penitentiary for many of the rapes. However, despite his many confessions of attacks, there are still quite a few cases that remain unsolved, and Bernardo has denied involvement in them.

Strangely enough, both Bernardo and Williams attended the same economics program and, in fact, Bernardo finished only one year behind him. There was a report in the Toronto Sun Newspaper that suggested Paul Bernardo and Williams not only went to the same classes, but also were friends and hung out together. However, Russell's best friend, Jeff Farquhar, has since denied that, saying, "If Russell had known Bernardo, I would have too!"

After studying economics for four years, Russell suddenly

announced that he wanted to join the Air Force. He told his friend Farquhar "I think I want to be a pilot!" This left Farquhar in shock. He told *CBC*,

> "Where did that come from? I was a little bit concerned because he was taking it way over the top. I really thought he was trying to live like Tom Cruise in Top Gun. So did a lot of us. I knew Russ well, and I thought, he's really lost in a fantasy world here, and I kept thinking to myself, oh, no, now he's going to be a jet fighter?"

In years to come, Russell would make his fantasy a reality, becoming one of Canada's top pilots, not only flying fighter jets but transport planes to war zones and natural disasters and carrying the Prime Minister and the Queen of England across the country and around the world.

Through it all, Russell remained friends with Farquhar and was even the emcee at his wedding. But there were some things Russell didn't share with his friend, like his impending marriage. "It was a complete shock to me," Farquhar said. "I mean, I was excited for him, but he hadn't been dating from university days, say from second year on." On June 1, 1991, Russell married Mary Elizabeth Harriman, who was the Associate Director of the Heart and Stroke Foundation of Canada.

Mary Elizabeth Harriman was born on November 15, 1957, the only daughter of Frederick and Irene Harriman. She also had a brother named Peter who died as an infant.

Harriman's father Frederick was a decorated military veteran who had spent five years overseas during the Second World War. He came back to study geology at the University of New Brunswick and later worked in mining exploration in Newfoundland, Quebec, and Northern Ontario.

Her mother, Irene Lavigne, had been a stenographer at a mining company in RouynNoranda, Quebec. Mary Elizabeth grew up in Madsen, Ontario, which was a rough mining town.

Mary was a student at the Red Lake District High School, where she graduated with honors. She then went to the University of Guelph in Ontario and graduated with a Bachelor of Science in 1980. She later attended St. Francis Xavier University to get her Masters in Education.

It was sometime in the late 1980s when Mary must have been introduced to Russell Williams. Harriman was five years older than Russell, but the two seemed to get along well.

The couple moved to Orleans, Ontario, which is a suburb of Ottawa, the capital of Canada. Williams had now been posted as Directorate of Air Requirements at the National Defense Headquarters. He served at the Airlift Capability Projects Strategic, Tactical, and Fixed-Wing Search and Rescue. In 1994, he was then posted to the 412 Transport Squadron in Ottawa, where he transported VIPs, including high-ranking government officials and foreign dignitaries. Williams was promoted to Major in 1999 and was posted to Director General Military Careers in Ottawa, where he served as the multi-engine pilot career manager.

Williams obtained his Master of Defense Studies from the Royal Military College of Canada in 2004 with a 55-page thesis that supported preemptive war in Iraq, and in July of 2004, he was promoted to Lieutenant Colonel. From there, he was moved to Camp Mirage, a secretive logistics facility believed to be located at Al Mirage Air Force Base in Dubai, United Arab Emirates that provides support to Canadian Forces operations in Afghanistan, where he served as commanding officer for seven months.

The commanding officer of Canada's Air Force at that time was Lieutenant General Angus Watt. Now retired, the General says that,

> "even under the constant scrutiny and evaluation of military life, Williams was one of the best and brightest, usually calm, very logical, very rational, and was able to produce good quality staff work in a fairly short time, which is a valued commodity in Ottawa."

Williams was promoted to Colonel on the recommendation of Lieutenant General Watt.

On July 15, 2009, Williams was sworn in as the Wing Commander at the Canadian Forces Base Trenton by the outgoing Wing Commander, Brigadier General Mike Hood. CFB Trenton is Canada's busiest air transport base and focus of support for overseas military operations. Located in Trenton, Ontario, the base also functions as the point of arrival for the bodies of all Canadian Air Force personnel killed in Afghanistan and is the starting point for funeral processions along the "Highway of Heroes" when their bodies are brought in for autopsies in Toronto.

Williams had flown Queen Elizabeth II and the Duke of Edinburgh, the Governor General of Canada, the Prime Minister of Canada, and many other dignitaries across Canada and overseas in Canadian Air Force VIP aircraft.

WELCOME TO OUR TOWN

"We live in a world that has narrowed into a neighborhood before it has broadened into a brotherhood." – Lyndon B. Johnson

Russell Williams and his wife bought a cottage located in Tweed, Ontario. This was to save Russell from driving back and forth from their Ottawa home to Trenton Air Force Base five days a week.

It was on a weekend in the Fall 2007 when a series of unusual break-ins began to unfold in and around Tweed. Russell Williams was at his cottage and neighbor Larry Jones was at home next door when he got frantic phone call from his daughter who lived nearby. She'd come home from a party and surprised an intruder in jogging clothes.

> "Christine opened the door to go from the garage into the house and saw this long, tall figure run past the door on the deck and jump over the fence and run off in the bush."

She thought it was just one of the neighborhood kids and nothing seemed to be missing. It would be years before the police told her something different. In fact, it would be years until anyone put together what had happened, beginning in 2007 when Russell Williams was at his cottage in Tweed; a multitude of bizarre break-ins with women's lingerie and underwear stolen, almost all of them occurred in his own neighborhood, especially on Cosy Cove Lane.

It was the same pattern as the break-ins in the nearby Ottawa suburb of Orleans, which were sometimes so well executed they weren't even noticed. We can't possibly know exactly what went on in each of the homes that Williams broke into, or what caused him to commit these bizarre crimes. Some believe it was the drugs, like Prednisone, that he was taking to relieve the pain that he was in from arthritis.

Several of the invasions he recorded, with photos or by

camcorder, and kept for himself, and eventually they were found by the police. These photos and recordings show us what sort of things he did during his invasions into other people's homes.

On the night of Saturday, September 8, 2007, Ron and Monique Murdoch, Williams's next door neighbors on Cozy Cove Lane, had to leave town with their two children to visit Monique's gravely ill mother in Sudbury, Ontario, which was about a six-hour drive from their home.

Williams had gotten to know the Murdoch family very well over the past few years. Quite often, he had been invited over for dinner and played cards with them until late in the night. Their daughter, Samantha, who was 12 years-old at the time, even showed Williams how to play crib and baked muffins for him. What made him decide to choose their house we will probably never know. Knowing that his neighbors had gone for at least a couple of nights, I suppose the Colonel just couldn't resist the empty house.

About 9:30 p.m., he crept across the dark yard and let himself in through an unlocked rear door. He headed straight for Samantha's bedroom where he started taking photos with his camera. The pictures started out with broad, general pictures of the whole room, but soon narrowed in on her dresser drawers. More specifically, her underwear drawers. Soon after that, he moved to her closet and took pictures of her clothes that were hanging, and then took pictures of her bed.

Sometime after he finished taking that series of pictures, he removed all his clothes. He then put on a pair of Samantha's pink panties and posed for some portraits, focusing on his protruding penis. He continued taking more pictures, like a photo shoot. He would pose in front of her mirror, hanging her pink panties from his erect penis. He then moved to her bed, where he lay naked, with his legs spread, and started to masturbate. He took plenty of time to set up his tripod and adjust different angles to get shots he must have found exciting. He then tried on more of the girl's panties, and even her training bras. He is thought to have spent about three hours there that night, and had taken several photos that clearly showed his ejaculation all over Samantha's underwear and bras.

When the Murdochs returned from their trip, they noticed nothing out of the ordinary and certainly had no reason to; after all, they had the most trusted man in the community taking care of their house. The crime remained unknown for some time. Three weeks later, Monique's mother passed away and the funeral was planned for Saturday, September 29, 2007, so the family was off again to Sudbury, Ontario.

Williams would take this opportunity to break into their house again. He entered through the same back door, only this time it was about 11:30 p.m., and he went directly to the girl's room again. He was much quicker this time, as he knew what he wanted to do. He removed all his clothes, set up his camera, and this time grabbed her panties and other garments from the dirty laundry basket.

Already erect by this time, he started to pose in front of the bedroom mirror, this time not only wearing different pairs of panties, but also her skirts and bras. It didn't take long for him to get erect, so while removing each garment, he would hang it over his penis and take another picture. Again he would masturbate, leave his ejaculate on her panties, and take pictures of that as well.

When the Murdochs returned, they again noticed nothing out of the ordinary. Williams soon came over to offer his condolences. He acted normal, and they felt no awkwardness around him at all.

It was in October, just a few weeks later, when Williams struck again. This time, it was a different neighbor. He picked Larry Jones's daughter's house, who had twin daughters herself, age 11 at the time. During the evening's festivities, he had much the same pattern. He would take several photos of the girls' room, the mother's room, and their underwear drawers, and even clothes that were inside the dryer. Williams stole a total of 23 pairs of underwear from all three females. Later, pictures were found of the girls' underpants spread out across his cottage floor in different types of display, almost like a catalog.

In total, Williams committed this same type of invasion 82 times in 48 different homes. Thirteen of the targets were females under the age of 18. It must be said that most of these break-ins remained unknown at the time; in fact, only one break-in was reported in Tweed and only 15 in Orleans out of the 48 homes that were broken into.

A year later, in June of 2008, was the first escalation in the items he would take from houses. In this case, he stole a sex toy that belonged to the 24-year-old resident, in addition to her undergarments.

In October of 2008, he upped his risk level even more.

Until now, he seemed to have been proud of the fact that he had done so many break-ins which the victims had not even realized, and he had not been discovered. But this time, it would be different. Williams broke into a house in Ottawa where a family with three girls lived. In one of the girl's rooms, he had taken her photo album out, opened it to a page of her own pictures, and left it on her bed. In another girl's room, he scattered a bunch of her 4x6 pictures of herself across her bedroom floor, and in the 12-year-old girl's room, he logged into her computer, looked through her pictures, and left a message: "Merci".

Williams continued to up the stakes of his crimes. Later that year, he broke into the house of a family that included a 15-year-old girl. He headed straight to her room, as he did on his other invasions, but this time he found a pair of her panties that had a blood stain on them. This apparently aroused him so much that he took pictures of himself licking the stain on the panties as well as wearing them over his face like a mask, and finally masturbating on the stain. In all, he took over 70 pictures of that visit. While the girl later realized that several of her panties were missing, the parents did not report it to the police, thinking it was just a prank being played on her by her step-siblings.

On January 1, 2009, New Year's Day, Brenda Constantine, her husband Brian Rogers, and their 15-year-old daughter were away in Toronto when Williams committed his first break-in at their home. He took several photos of the girl's bedroom, removed all the underwear from her drawers and took them home with him. He was rather quick, far less than an hour, not his usual visit. He returned the next night, but this time he must have been far more comfortable, as he stripped down naked as soon as he arrived. He then followed his normal ritual by taking photos of himself both naked and dressed in the girl's clothing.

In one of the photos, he took the girl's make-up brush and brushed it along his erect penis several times. He then put the brush back for her to use again. This night, instead of taking just panties and bras, he also took some dresses, a tank top, and even shoes.

Later in an interview on CBC's *The Fifth Estate*, the family described their ordeal, saying soon after they got home from their trip, their teenage girl was unpacking and noticed something strange. Brenda said, "My daughter came running down the stairs, telling us that all her underwear was gone out of her drawer, and we kind of laughed and said 'check the floor' because you know how teenagers are, check the laundry or whatever. She said, no, I'm serious, there's nothing left in my drawers!"

Brenda Constantine and her husband Brian Rogers would start to take their daughter's claims much more seriously when their daughter also discovered what else was missing. "She went back upstairs to realize there [were] dresses, shoes, and all of her bathing suits and even photographs of herself gone." Someone had gone through their family albums, selecting pictures of their 15-year-old daughter, and police found something even more disturbing. "They did tell us that they took some DNA evidence from my daughter's bedroom from around her bureau, where the underwear drawer was, around that area," Brenda said. "They wanted us to wash everything clean and, of course, my daughter didn't want to sleep in her bedroom for three months."

This must have been very terrifying for the family, as somebody was obviously targeting their 15-year-old girl. "We wouldn't let her go anywhere or do anything alone," Brenda continued. "She wasn't allowed to stay home alone and her brothers were basically her bodyguards, and we had friends looking out for her as well."

After speaking to the police, the family learned of the other break-ins in the area with similar thefts, so they decided to call a town meeting. Even though the heat was on and the police were looking for a serial thief, Williams would continue his series of many more home invasions. He would keep the same patterns, only taking more pieces of clothing in each case. In some cases, he would take as many as 168 pieces just from one person.

When Williams took command in Trenton, the demands on him increased. He was now responsible for thousands of military men and women and was often in the public eye. Following his promotion in July 2009, per police records the frequency of the break-ins increased, too. There were ten more in his first two months as Wing Commander, and all the while Colonel Williams performed his official duties.

THE FIRST ASSAULT

It was only a few hours after Williams returned home from his trip to Alaska when he committed his first physical assault on a woman. It was September 17, 2009. He had selected a young woman whose name remains unknown to the public. He probably spotted her on one of his many jogs around the area, which is how he learned about his victims' living arrangements and lifestyles. Even now, the victim's name still has not been released, even after she later had won a civil lawsuit against Williams. We will call the unknown woman "victim" for the story of the assault.

The victim had just moved to a house on Cosy Cove Lane with her boyfriend and infant daughter just one month prior. She had just left her husband and decided to move to where her new boyfriend had grown up.

The victim's boyfriend would travel for work with a utilities company and leave her alone with her baby at the house. She had not had much of a chance to get to know any of her neighbors yet because she had so much to do with her baby and setting up the new home for her family.

On the night of the assault, the victim had been visiting her mother's house and didn't get home until about 9:30 p.m. She put her baby to bed right away, as it was late, and she cleaned her house a little. About an hour and a half later, she went to bed and fell asleep within minutes.

The next thing she remembered was being hit on the left side of her head. At first, she thought she was dreaming, but the hits kept on coming, so she reached up into the air and grabbed what seemed to be a man towering over her.

The man then laid down on top of her and started to press down on her face hard with his right-hand palm. She was terrified and immediately thought of her baby daughter asleep in the next room.

Victim: "How did you get in? What time is it? The baby is sure to wake up crying at 4 a.m."

Williams: "It's only 1 a.m., don't worry." He then had to pick up his herringbone chain off the bed, as it had been torn off in the struggle, and put it into his pants pocket.

Victim: "Are you going to kill me afterwards?"

Williams: "No!"

Victim: "Promise and everything? I'll do whatever you want, just please don't hurt me or the baby." She started to pull her bottoms off with her free hand, but Williams slapped her arm. "We can just talk, if you like? You really don't seem like a bad person. Not like the type of person who would do something like this. Do you work?"

Williams: "No."

Victim: "Do you get bored like me? I get pretty bored looking after the baby around here all day. You must live around here, right?"

Williams was not answering her questions; he was just focused on what he wanted to do. "Roll over on your tummy." And as she did, he moved to climb on top of her buttocks. He then pressed down on her back with one hand and struck her three times on the back of her head with the other, telling her,

"Be quiet, and don't ever try to look at my face!"

She became quiet and began to lay still, not struggling.

>Williams: "Where's Dad?"
>
>Victim: "How do you know there's a dad? I could be a single mother."
>
>Williams: "How long have you lived here?"
>
>Victim: "Just a month. My boyfriend's family was from here, but I really don't like it here, the town's way too small."
>
>Williams: "What's your name?"
>
>Victim: "Allison," she lied.
>
>Williams: "I need to control you better!" Just then he started to grab the pillowcases. "Keep your arms behind you!"
>
>Victim: "I won't let you tie me up!"

He then got a little rough with her and placed a blanket over her arms. He placed both knees on top of it. While she struggled to get free, the intruder started to rip the pillow cases into strips and began to tie her wrists. Once her hands were secured, he pulled another full pillowcase over her head, and secured it using a rubber band around her neck.

Williams made her stand up and he guided her to the living room where he had a bag sitting on the floor. He started to rummage through the bag.

Victim: "What is that? What's happening?"

Williams: "You'll see." Then Williams walked her back to her bedroom and sat her down on the bed. "But don't worry, I'm not going to rape you and I won't hurt you either. I've got a camera here."

The victim heard a beeping noise and could see a light through the pillowcase over her head.

Victim: "You've taken my picture? I'm not really very attractive since having my baby. The pregnancy packed on a lot of fat."

Williams: "I think you're perfect." He then took out her left breast from her top, and took a picture. Then he took out the right breast, and took another picture. He then pulled her camisole down to where it rested on her waist. He continued to fondle her breasts and take more pictures.

Williams: "Stand up and pull down your pants!"

Victim: "You promised you weren't going to rape me!"

Williams: "I'm not, just do as I say." He then pulled her pajama bottoms down to her feet and kicked them away into the middle of the floor. Williams then pushed her onto the bed and forced her to spread her legs and took some more pictures. Five minutes passed and then the intruder left the room quickly.

Victim: "Am I doing anything wrong?"

She screamed loudly so he could hear her. "Should I be doing anything differently?"

Williams returned to her room and started to rifle through her dresser drawers. All of a sudden, it became quiet for a few minutes, until she heard him speak again.

Williams: "Now stand up." She could hear the intruder removing all the sheets and blankets from her bed.

Victim: "Please don't leave me without any clothes on."

Williams then guided her towards the bedroom wall and had her lean up against it. He started to dress her now, putting her pajama bottoms back on her first. He then covered her top section up with the camisole she was wearing before.

Victim: "May I go check on my baby?"

Williams didn't say a word, he just grabbed her by the arm, and firmly led her to the baby's room. He then walked her up to the baby crib and allowed her to lean over and touch her baby's face with her lips.

Williams then touched her breasts again.

Williams: "Count to 300 before removing your blindfold." She began counting and when she got to 70, she stopped, thinking that he must be gone now as it had remained silent the whole time.

Williams: "Keep going!" she started counting again.

This time, she counted until she reached 200 and then stopped and yelled out to see if he would answer. After hearing nothing, she took off her blindfold, grabbed her baby, and ran to the phone. She first called her boyfriend's mother and told her of the attack. After her family told her they would be right over, she hung up and called 911.

The first people to arrive at her home was her boyfriend's mother, brother, and some other male that she didn't recognize. Her boyfriend's mother ran into the house and put her arms around her, while the men searched through the house and around the lawns. They found her sliding door open, but they couldn't tell if that's how he got in or how he left.

It wasn't much longer before the Ontario Provincial Police showed up and searched the area as well. When the police checked with her neighbors, none of them reported hearing anything at all. The victim had not heard anything before her attack.

It was 7:30 a.m. before the forensics unit showed up and collected the pillowcases and all the items the intruder had used on her. They also took swabs from the victim's bedrooms.

The victim was able to give a fairly good description even though she was blindfolded and tied up. But later, we would know this would be unreliable. She described her intruder as between the ages of 30 and 50, that he seemed like a dad, was not very tall, maybe 5' 2", average build, no facial hair, and had no eyeglasses on or anything covering his face.

He also wore a tight sweater, which she claimed to have torn during their struggle. He also wore hiking boots, he smelled dirty, and had a ring on one of his fingers as well. After her interview, she left town and moved to the city of Belleville. She never returned. Her boyfriend went to the house and collected all of her personal belongings.

3

MISTAKEN IDENTITY

It was on the night of September 30, 2009, at about 1 a.m. when a loud crash in Laurie's house abruptly woke her from a dead sleep. Laurie sat up quickly with her face still covered by her comforter. She was so startled she had to catch her breath. Suddenly, she felt something smash her in the side of her head. Struggling to try and gain her composure, there were three more hard blows to her head.

Laurie screamed out, "What's happening?!"

Then a cold, assertive male voice answered her. "Don't you realize what's going on?" She felt a strong hand wrap its fingers around her throat. "You're being cleaned out. Shhh, I need you to be quiet. Don't make a sound." Laurie could feel the weight of the man's body press against her, and the man's grip became so strong around her throat she could feel her face get hot and her blood trying to flow through her neck.

Laurie then managed to get out the words "Please don't, I can't breathe," while trying to get some air. She began to cry and continued to try to talk. "I have children, they can't find me like this. Please don't do this to me, please."

The intruder let Laurie lay back onto the bed, still leaving the comforter over her face.

"It's my job to control you. Don't dare challenge my authority; this is going to take a while."

The sound of the TV playing a show filled the air for several minutes, then the intruder started to tell Laurie about the plan to rob her house, and how it was planned to happen the day before, only somebody else had shown up at her house.

Intruder: "Who was it that visited you last night?"

Laurie: "Nobody." Still quite nervous, Laurie decided she could get rid of her burglars faster if she helped them find what they were looking for. "I can tell you where my rings are, they are diamond."

Intruder: "They'll take whatever they're going to take. Where's your family? Is anyone going to show up here?"

Laurie: "Oh God, no, nobody can stand me. I don't have a family, even my boyfriend can't stand me."

Intruder: "Will you promise to give us a half an hour to get away?"

Laurie: "Yes, of course I will, you're not as bad as those other guys, at least you're not stealing like them."

She then began to ask if she could sit up. "Do you smoke?"

Intruder: "No. I'll let you sit up, but trust me, you don't want to see me!"

Laurie then sat up slowly, making sure to keep the comforter over her face. "Maybe you could blindfold me instead?" She then started to rip material from her Winnie the Pooh pillow that lay beside her on the bed. "Here, you can use some of this material."

Intruder: "I'll take care of that." He grabbed the pillow from her and began to cut off pieces of material with a knife.

After the tearing noises stopped, she could feel the intruder come up behind her and slowly remove the comforter from her face. Laurie kept her eyelids tightly closed to make sure she didn't catch any glimpse of the man. The man slowly tied the pieces of material around her face covering her eyes.

| Laurie Massicote

While he was tying the material around her head, he had caught some of her blonde hair, and because he secured it so tightly, the hair had clumped, causing Laurie to let out a shriek.

Intruder: "Okay. Let me see if I can fix that for you." He then slowly pulled the hair that was stuck out from under the blindfold. "Is that better?"

Laurie: "Yes, thank you."

The intruder then took the pillow and ripped some more material from it. He then tied Laurie's hands behind her back with it. "Can't have loose hands, that would just give you too much control, and the others wouldn't like that very much."

The intruder got up off of the bed and said, "I have to go check on the others." He left the room and moments later she heard him yell out from the other room, "Are you looking at me?"

Laurie: "God, no." She put her head down quickly. Laurie then heard the man walk down the hallway away from her room.

Five minutes later, she could hear the man come back into her room. Laurie said, "I have a really, really bad pounding headache. Do you think you could get me some Tylenol?"

Intruder: "Sure, where do I find them?"

Laurie: "They are in the bathroom at the end of my hallway, in the medicine cabinet."

The intruder came back with the Tylenol and asked, "How are you going to take them? You'll need some water."

Laurie: "There's a coffee cup on my end table right there.

It's got an apple core in it; you can just throw it away and use that cup."

Intruder: "All right, but I'm going to have to take you along to get this water." The intruder then pulled her down the hallway into the bathroom. She stood in front of the sink and he filled her cup with water so that she could take her pills. After she finished drinking the water, he wanted to know if she needed to use the bathroom.

Laurie: "That's alright, I've already gone." She pointed her head towards her pajama bottoms. She had lost control when he first came into her room and began to choke her. The intruder then walked her back to her room and she sat down on the bed. He began to rub her temples and told her he was sorry.

The intruder then left the room for a while and returned with another cup of water and some more pills. "Here, take these, they are Tylenol, trust me." She took them and started to drink the water he had brought in to her, only she thought the water had a bad taste; it wasn't anything like what she just drank a few minutes earlier.

She could then feel his weight on the bed, as he sat down beside her. "Here, take another drink."

Laurie: "This water tastes funny." He never answered her. "Please, can I just have my arms free? These ties are really hurting me, and my wrists are throbbing."

Intruder: "I can't untie you, but maybe I can do something to loosen them up. But I'd need some more material."

Laurie: "In that room right behind you, you'll find whatever you need in there, sheets, pillowcases, whatever." The man left the room and she could hear him shuffle through things. Finally, he came back and sat beside her, as she could feel the pressure on the seat cushion from his body weight. He then moved her so that her wrists were facing him.

Intruder: "Now stay still, so I don't cut either of us." Then he cut through her wrist bindings with his knife. As soon as her wrists became free, he grabbed them and placed them behind her back and tied them up again with a pillowcase and some large cables. He was much nicer than he had been earlier and didn't tie them with as much tension. "I'm trying to make this as comfortable as possible for you. Is this okay?" Laurie then nodded her head in approval and said nothing. The intruder suddenly jumped to his feet and said loudly, "I thought you said that nobody was here. What's that I hear?"

Laurie: "I've got two cats, it must be one of them."

The intruder let out a loud sigh of relief and sat back down beside Laurie on the bed. He then picked up the cup of water he was making her drink from before and told her to drink some more. She took a couple more drinks when another noise came from the basement. "What's that?" the intruder said as he rose to his feet once more.

Laurie: "That's got to be another one of my cats." Just then, one of her cats came out of nowhere and jumped onto her lap. The intruder sat back down. Laurie moved her body enough to knock the cat off of her lap. "Sorry, honey, you're going to have to get off my lap, because this gentleman is allergic to cats."

Intruder: "That's okay. Hey, this is a pretty nice house, how do you pay for it?"

Laurie: "Borrowed money. So do you have a wife and children?"

Intruder: "No!" he said loudly.

Laurie: "So, why not?"

Intruder: "I'm too young." The intruder then stood up and walked out of the room.

About five minutes passed before he came back into the room, Laurie sensed that the man was breathing much heavier and fast now. "What's wrong?" she asked.

Intruder: "Nothing."

Laurie then started to think about how her ex-husband had offered some money to one of their friends to scare her by doing a home invasion on her. She began wondering if he had found someone to do this and this was what was happening to her now. The sound of her TV going off snapped her from her thoughts. She then heard her bamboo blinds rattle and slam as each of them were being lowered and closed.

Next, she felt the intruder sit down beside her again, only this time she heard a zipper open. "What are you doing? Do you have a gun? Oh, my God, you're going to kill me, aren't you?"

Intruder: "No, Laurie, I'm not going to kill you. I've got a camera. I just want to take a couple of pictures of you."

Laurie: "Take pictures, why would you want to take pictures of me?"

Intruder: "So that you know we have pictures of you."

Laurie: "Is that honestly all you have is a camera? Is there a gun? I know you're going to kill me, aren't you?"

The intruder rubbed the camera strap against her cheek. "You see, it's just a camera." He then placed the camera down near her hands so that she could feel it. "You see, calm down, okay?"

Laurie next noticed the red light of the camera as the intruder started to take pictures of her. After he took three or four pictures, he sat down beside her again. "I want to take some more pictures. But I'll need to pull your shirt up first." Laurie felt the intruder slowly pull her shirt up until it rested on her shoulders around her neck. He stood up again and started to take more pictures of her.

When he finished taking the pictures, he sat down beside her again. He then took his left hand and moved it across her chest and under her bra, where he cupped her breast firmly.

Laurie: "Oh, my God, please don't." He took his hand away.

Intruder: "You've got very nice breasts." Laurie shook her head no.

Intruder: "Yes, you do, you're beautiful." He then slid his hand underneath her bra again and cupped her breast. She then screamed no, and he quickly removed his hand again.

Intruder: "Here, you can pull your shirt back down now." He assisted her with lowering her shirt back down to her waist. The man stood up and she could hear a quick slicing noise and suddenly she felt her shirt fall off her chest and into her hands in two pieces.

She heard him take some more pictures of her, then sit down beside her again. He then sliced the straps of the back of her bra and helped remove it from her. He started to feel her chest and stomach until he felt that she had a belly button ring on. He stood up and walked around until he faced her, and said, "Oh, that's nice..." he continued to play with her ring.

Laurie: "I've gone through some stuff lately, and I'm not sure if I'm pregnant or what."

Intruder: "How could that be? You're 47."

Laurie: "I'm not sure what's going on. Maybe it's menopause, but something funky is happening anyway." But the intruder kept caressing her stomach, then started to move his hand into the front of her pajama bottoms. "Oh, please don't do that, please don't!" Laurie screamed. Right away the intruder pulled his hand away. A few minutes later, he started to pull her pajama bottoms down again, and she continued to try and talk him out of it. "Please don't, this isn't good; I told you I had an accident." Then Laurie could hear the intruder taking the knife from his holder and she went quiet with fear. He then put the knife up against her stomach, so she began to remove her bottoms until they fell around her feet. The next thing she saw was the flashes of the camera when he started to take some more pictures. Laurie then tried to squat forward and contort her body to try and keep as much of her private parts covered as possible. He then grabbed her one leg firmly and started to try and move it in a pose. "Come on, put your leg up on the chair."

Laurie: "Why are you doing this?"

Intruder: "Because it has to be done." He continued to take photos of her, only this time they were up close shots of her genitals. "I'm running out of time. I'll be right back, I have to check on the others again." She then heard him leave the room.

Minutes later while sitting on the bed quietly so she could hear as much as possible, she heard what sounded like bullets being loaded into a chamber of a gun. "What's that? What's going on?" she said loudly so that he would hear her in the other room.

Intruder: "It's just the batteries, I have to recharge them." He then walked back into her room. "I have one more thing for you to do, stand up."

Laurie: "I can't stand up. You're going to kill me if I do."

Intruder: "Laurie, I'm not going to kill you."

Laurie slowly started to stand up. "Why are you doing this?"

Intruder: "So that I can get on with my life, and so can you. I want you to start turning around in a circle." As she started to move as he instructed her, he started to take more photos of her. He then told her to sit back down; after she did, he covered up with a comforter and told her that he had to go and check on the others again.

The house went silent for several minutes until he came back into her room and said, "There's just one more thing I need from you, Laurie."

Laurie: "You promised when you made me stand up that those would be the last pictures you were going to take."

Intruder: "I need one more thing from you and it'll all be over. I want you to get up on the bed on your hands and knees and put your head down."

Laurie: "Why? I can't do that, there's no way, I can't."

Intruder: "You've been cooperative so far, Laurie. You can do it, I know you can. Don't make me make you!"

Laurie: "I'm going to need some help getting into that position, I can't do it by myself."

The intruder walked over to her, lifted her up, and laid her on the bed face down. She slowly got into the position that he wanted her in. "God, now I know you have a gun and you're going to kill me."

Intruder: "Laurie, I told you there would be no need for that. I don't have a gun." He then walked around the bed, taking more photos of her. After he was through, he helped her get seated again and placed the comforter on top of her. He took two more photos of her while she was sitting on the bed, but this time he had his exposed penis in the pictures. She was not aware of that.

The intruder walked out of the room, and minutes later Laurie could hear some commotion in the kitchen.

Laurie: "What are you doing?"

Intruder: "I'm wiping my prints off this coffee cup that I touched earlier."

Laurie: "Well, you better wipe off the Tylenol bottle, too."

Intruder: "Oh yes, good thinking, Laurie."

As soon as he finished wiping all of the areas and items that he could remember touching, he went back into Laurie's bedroom and stole some underwear. He walked back to where Laurie was and said, "It's 4:30 in the morning now, and they're done here, so I'm going to leave now. I just want to make sure that you uphold your end of the bargain and they get out okay. So I'll be back in 10 minutes to check on you."

Laurie: "Before you go, would it be possible for me to have a cigarette, please?" She then felt a cigarette pressed into her lips and heard the man flicking a lighter, so she started to suck so that it would start.

About 10 minutes of silence went by before a loud crash occurred. Laurie thought it sounded like someone had driven into her garage door. She remained quiet and motionless. Laurie waited for another 15 minutes before deciding to try and escape. She started by rolling and sliding on the bed until her blindfold slid off of her head.

It took about another 10 minutes before Laurie was able to get free. She saw a cigarette on her floor, so she picked it up and lit it. She sat down and turned on her TV and planned what she would do next. After two cigarettes were smoked, she decided that she would call 911.

Operator: "911 emergency, what do you need, police, ambulance, or fire?"

Laurie: "I'm not really sure what happened here, apparently there were others, they were supposed to be robbing the place, and I just...this guy took pictures of me, and you know, I…"

Operator: "Do you know who it was?"

Laurie: "He blindfolded me. No, I didn't see a thing. I don't know if it was my ex-husband or who the heck this was. I have a weird feeling it was my ex-husband and some other men."

Operator: "Are you sure?"

Laurie: "I have no idea."

Operator: "The police are on their way, it won't be long."

Laurie: "They've been here before because of issues with my ex-husband, so they should be familiar with it. I'm sitting here and I'm really, really embarrassed right now. I don't want to have to go to the other end of the house to open the door for them. Can you please tell them to go around to the side door? I can unlock that one much faster when they get here."

Operator: "That's alright, stay where you are, and I'll stay on the line with you until they get there."

Five minutes later, the officers arrived and the operator told Laurie she could unlock her door now. Laurie stood up, still holding the comforter, and unlocked the door.

Laurie: "Can you please tell them to wait until I sit down

again, I'm still only partially clad." Laurie got seated on the floor again and waited. Soon the door opened and officers came into the room. "Hi, Laurie, how are you? Don't move, remain where you are."

The officers then asked Laurie if she could describe what items had been disturbed as the forensics unit from Belleville had been called and should be arriving in about 30 minutes. Laurie was then taken to the Ontario Provincial Police Central Hastings detachment where she was interviewed by detectives. It was during the interview that Laurie found out about another attack that had occurred on the same street that Laurie lived on, and it had happened only 12 days earlier.

The OPP had decided not to release the information about the attack on the woman 12 days prior as they didn't want to panic the city as they thought that it was going to be a single occurrence. There had also been rumors around town that the woman attacked had actually staged the event against the man she was having an affair with. People were suspicious that there had been no penetration during the attack. Locals added Laurie to that list as well, saying that she just wanted to get some government money from the victim compensation fund.

Police took to the neighborhood, going door to door. All residents were questioned, except for Colonel Russell Williams, as he was away from home when they were canvassing. The OPP officer decided not to return to Williams's home, as he was the commander of the 8 Wing Trenton Air Force Base.

The next day, the Ontario Provincial Police finally released their press release:

> "The Ontario Provincial Police, Central Hastings detachment, are investigating two break-ins that occurred during which a male suspect entered the home while the residents were sleeping. On September 17 and again on September 30, 2009, both in the early hours of the morning, an unknown male entered Tweed residences. During both separate incidents, the suspect struck the female victim, tied her to a chair, and took photos of her. The suspect then fled the scene. The OPP want to remind everyone to ensure all doors and windows are secured and to practice personal safety. Please report any suspicious activity to the police immediately by calling 911. OPP officers are following up leads to identify the suspect. If anyone has information about these incidents, they are asked to call the Central Hastings OPP."

Within a few days, Laurie Massicotte called Detective Constable Alexander and told him that after having taken some time to reflect on the attack and play back the words and type of conversations that she had with her attacker, she was now certain that she knew his identity. The intruder's voice had belonged to a man who lived only a few doors down from her named Larry Jones.

4

MURDER OF CORPORAL MARIE-FRANCE COMEAU

Corporal Marie-France Comeau was born into a military family in 1972. Her dad was a Canadian Armed Forces medic, and one of her grandfathers had earned honors as a pilot in World War II. Growing up listening to the war stories of both men greatly excited the young girl, who at an early age made an important decision. She would join the Air Force. She ended up among the crew that escorted Prime Minister Stephen Harper to Mumbai in November 2009. Now back from the trip that she had always dreamed about, she was looking forward to telling her boyfriend all about it.

However, while she was away, a predator had been on his own trip - to her home. One week before, knowing that she was away, Williams had made a reconnaissance trip to her home. He found the rear basement window unlocked. It was large enough for him to fit through. He checked out her bathroom and closets to make sure there were no signs of a man living there. He also couldn't resist the bedroom, where he would find her sex toys, bras, and panties, some of which he couldn't help but try on and even take with him to his own home.

It was 11 p.m. Williams had made the same trip to her house again and entered her home the same way that he had done the week previously. He was now in her basement, waiting for her to go to bed and fall asleep.

Marie-France was on the phone with her boyfriend, setting up dinner plans with him so that she could share all the events of her recent trip. After finishing her call, Marie-France realized she had not seen her cat, Bixby. Starting her search, she headed for the basement, knowing that was his favorite hiding spot. "Bixby, where are you?" she yelled from the top of the stairs. She turned on the basement lights, and started down the stairs to find her cat. "There you are!" She walked toward the cat and bent down to pick him up. As she did, she saw a dark figure behind the furnace and screamed loudly.

Knowing he must silence her right away, he smashed his flashlight over her head. This only made her want to fight, even though she could feel the blood on her head. It took several more blows before she would fall backwards. Williams then lunged on top of her, which smeared her blood across the cement floor. He bound her wrists with rope. He stood her up and pushed her against a metal jack support post, where a steel pin ripped into her upper back. He then tied her firmly to the post and covered her mouth with duct tape.

Now that his victim was secured, he would now make sure that they would not be interrupted. He took her house key, which had been left on the kitchen table, and snapped it off in the lock of the front door so that nobody who had a key could get in. He then headed for her bedroom, ripped the comforter off her bed, and covered her bedroom window with it.

He then headed back to the basement, not paying attention to the trail of blood that he was leaving with his shoes. He removed the duct tape from her mouth and cut the ties to the post so that he could bring her upstairs to the bedroom. While starting up the stairs, Marie-France started to scream. He quickly grabbed her head and smashed it against the wall, creating a spray of blood and a head-shaped crater. Marie-France now dropped to the floor unconscious.

Williams now felt compelled to get his camera and take four pictures of her lying naked and bleeding on the floor, including a close-up on her vagina and the cuts on her breasts and face. Williams then carried her up to her bedroom, placed her onto the bed, and placed her in a fetal position. He grabbed a towel from the bathroom and wrapped it around her head, covering her eyes and nose, then wrapped it with duct tape to keep it in place. He then set up his camcorder on a tripod at the foot of the bed, focusing on the still unconscious Marie-France, pressed "RECORD," and started to undress.

He climbed onto the bed wearing nothing except on his face, which was covered with a black skull cap. He forced Marie-France onto her back, spread her legs, and lined her up for penetration. She then moaned as he began to rape her. He grabbed his camera, which he had placed on the bed, and started taking pictures of the penetration. After 17 minutes of raping her in several different positions, only stopping to take random pictures, Williams then removed his face mask, and smiled smugly at the camcorder while rubbing her breasts and stomach.

All the while, Marie-France was telling him, "Get out! I want you to leave," but he didn't answer. Williams then whispered, "Stay there," and again got up from the bed, smiled into the camcorder, and grabbed and squeezed some KY jelly onto his fingers. He moved back towards the bed, applied the lubricant to her genitals, and climbed back on top of her. After a few more minutes of intercourse, he looked back into the camera, withdrew, and carefully caught his ejaculate into his cupped hand.

Now on his way into the bathroom, she wondered if she could try and escape. Hearing the toilet flush, she slid herself off the bed. She heard Williams walk into the living room, so she headed for the bathroom and slammed the door closed behind her, hoping to get the door locked behind her before he noticed she was no longer on the bed. She wasn't fast enough. He smashed through the door and threw her against the bathroom wall. He grabbed her by the hair and dragged her back into the bedroom, pushing her into a seated position on the bed. "Now stay here!" he told her boldly. He forced intercourse on her again, followed by another round of photographs.

After he finished, Williams then rifled through her drawers, taking out select pieces of underwear and laying them onto her body, then took more pictures. It was like he wanted to model her in different garments to create a

MURDER OF CORPORAL MARIE-FRANCE COMEAU | 47

catalog for himself. He then started placing them into his duffel bag, perhaps as souvenirs that he could have for future benefit to relieve himself with.

She then began to moan loudly and move back and forth on the bed. He quickly lay down beside her and told her to be quiet. "No, please…" she replied. "I don't want to die."

"You're not going to die," Williams answered quickly, and the struggle went on like this back and forth for several minutes.

He then placed more duct tape around her face, covering her mouth and nose this time. According to the police transcripts, she then died of suffocation due to her airways being covered with duct tape.

It was now 4 a.m. and he had to be at an important meeting in Ottawa, about a three-hour drive away, so Williams had no time to go home. Before leaving, he threw all the sheets from her bed and the comforter that he had hung over the window into the wash and doused them in bleach. He did not realize that he had left his shoe print in the trail of blood — mistake that would soon catch up to him.

The next morning, November 25, Comeau's boyfriend became worried as she had not shown up for work. He had just spoken to her the previous night, and this was very unlike Marie-France. He then went over to her home and let himself in. Outside, Comeau's neighbor, Terry Alexander, had a plumber who had come to his house for repairs.

He recalls Marie-France's boyfriend suddenly bursting out of the home, running across the street, tears running down his face. "Did you see any strange people or cars around here?" he shouted. "She's lying dead inside!" he said before breaking down into sobs.

Investigations concluded two days later that Comeau's death had been a homicide.

Investigators from Northumberland OPP (Ontario Provincial Police) spent a few weeks looking for evidence, even stripping the floors down to the concrete and ripping out the cabinets in the kitchen.

The neighbors in the small town were afraid, and rumors began to spread, many having different theories on the events that had taken place. Many neighbors had not known her well. Terry Alexander spoke of her shyness, and another neighbor said that he had never seen her around the block.

Her ex-boyfriend, Alain Plante, who was a basic training instructor, had spent more than four years with her, and his son Etienne had loved the woman like his mother.

The funeral of Marie France-Comeau

The Corporal was buried on December 4, 2009, at the National Military Cemetery in Ottawa. Many family members, fellow military officers, and friends attended the ceremony. An ironic and perhaps angering fact is that as her commanding officer, Williams was tasked with writing an official letter of condolence to her father. He also attended the funeral and participated, reading the eulogy for Comeau, who nobody could have imagined been murdered by the Colonel himself.

MURDER OF JESSICA LLOYD

Jessica Lloyd was a 27-year-old brunette with green eyes who loved to smile and lived alone in a red brick bungalow on a desolate stretch of rural Highway 37 between Belleville and Tweed. She was really into fitness and would often exercise on her treadmill in her basement with her curtains wide open. Jessica worked at the Tri-Board Student Transportation Services where she was the administrator of a school bus line. Friends and family members described her as outgoing, popular, and close with her loved ones who she talked to daily.

One morning in late January 2010, Russell was running along the highway when he spotted her. She was exercising on her treadmill in the basement. Williams stopped and pretended to be tying his shoes. He watched her for a while, becoming sexually aroused at the sight of her.

It would be a few nights later, on January 28, while driving by her home, that he had noticed the absence of her car. He pulled off the rural highway into a vacant lot that was situated beside her home. It was total darkness, but a clear full moon was out that evening, making it easy to find his way through the field to her home. He found the rear sliding glass patio door unlocked, and he let himself into the house. The interior was dark, but he had his flashlight, so he decided to prowl around carefully and get to know the layout of the house.

As previously with Marie-France Comeau, he made his way through the bathroom and closets to make sure that there were no men living there. Having assured himself that Jessica lived alone, he left the house and made his way back through the field to his vehicle.

Around 9 p.m. that night, he saw a car pull into the driveway. Somebody got out of the driver's side of the car and went to the front door. After a few minutes, whoever it was got back into their car and left.

Then at about 10:30 p.m., he saw another car pull into the driveway. He waited to make sure it was Jessica and that she was alone. It wasn't long before she made her way to bed, and the house became dark.

He quietly made his way back into the house through the same back patio door that he had used earlier. He covered his face with the same black skull cap that he had used before. When he entered her bedroom, he saw her lying still, and he was sure she was already asleep. Williams moved towards her with his flashlight ready to strike her unconscious when Jessica's eyes suddenly opened. "Don't scream," he warned her. "Lie on your tummy." He ordered. Totally frightened, she froze. She rolled over, and he tied her hands with rope behind her back. "Keep your eyes shut. You don't want to see me." He pulled her up on her feet.

He led Jessica out into the hallway, where he stopped to take some photos. He then wrapped duct tape around her eyes and placed her back on her bed, securing her tied hands to the headboard. He set up his camcorder at the foot of the bed, just as he had done before in Comeau's house, aimed it at Jessica, and started filming. Taking a military-grade knife from his duffel bag, he slashed through her thin top, exposing her breasts. He then removed her panties, grabbed the camcorder, and started to film up and down her body.

He then gave her the command to spread her legs, bend her knees, and open her mouth, and he continued to film. "Now close them." Her reluctance was obvious. "You want to survive this, don't you?" he exclaimed.

"Yes!" she replied.

"Okay, good," he said reassuringly while he removed his own clothing. He took more close-up pictures, and asked her, "why do you shave your pussy?"

"I don't know, I just do, I have for a while." She answered. He continued to pose her in a variety of positions while he continued to take pictures.

Williams then removed two black plastic zip ties from his bag and fastened them tight around her neck. "What do you think is happening now?"

"I don't know," she replied. While holding the camcorder, he walked towards Jessica and tugged on the black ties.

"You feel that?" She nodded. "If I feel something I don't like, I pull on that, and you die. You got it? Do you want to die?" She shook her head no. "Open your mouth." He then focused the camera on her terrified face. He then forced his penis into her mouth, still holding the black ties in his hand. He would then force her to continue the fellatio, pausing only to take pictures. Minutes later, he reached orgasm, and forced her to swallow his ejaculate.

A few minutes later, Williams was startled by a noise. He left the bedroom to go look around for the source of the noise. He then asked her if she had a cat, and she said she didn't. Williams returned to the room and got himself quickly dressed. He then helped Jessica get dressed by selecting a pair of jeans, a hoodie, and a brown pair of shoes. He had decided to change his plans and take Jessica back to his place.

He then led her across the dark field. She still had the towel and duct tape wrapped around her face. He placed her into the front passenger seat of his truck and drove the 25 minutes back to his home. It was now 4:30 a.m. Before he continued doing what he was doing with her earlier, he insisted that she take a shower. He helped her get undressed and put her into the shower. Before he climbed into the shower with her, he set up his camcorder to record the event.

After he finished with her in the shower, he dried her off and led her into his bedroom, placed her in bed, and tied a rope around both of their wrists so that she couldn't leave the bed without waking him. After they slept for a few hours, she woke Williams up by convulsing and asking him to take her to the hospital. It seemed to startle Williams. He removed the ropes from her wrist and helped her pull her pants and sweater on. He sat on the bed beside her and started rubbing her head as if to calm her. "If I die, will you make sure my mom knows that I love her?" Jessica asked him.

We don't know what happened next, as the camera was stopped. The next time the camera was started again, Jessica was still fully clothed and sleeping on the floor. Her plan to get medical help had failed. Over the next several hours, he then made her wear different pairs of panties and bras while he took pictures of her in directed poses that he would suggest.

He then told Jessica that it was time to go and he would safely drop her back at her home. She walked ahead of him, still blindfolded, into his cold garage. Just before getting into his truck, he smashed her over the head with his flashlight to render her unconscious. Instead, she collapsed to the floor with a large pool of blood surrounding her head. She was still breathing, so he took the rope and tied it around her neck and pulled it tightly until her body went limp.

His first impulse was to go get his camera and take pictures of the freshly killed woman. Shortly after he took the pictures, he had to get dressed and ready to go to work. He was scheduled for 5:30 a.m., so he planned to dispose of the body later. He then placed the corpse of Jessica Lloyd in his garage before dumping it on a road a short way from his cottage, taking note of the exact location. A few hours later, he piloted a troop flight to California.

On the morning of Friday, January 29, fellow employees realized that Lloyd had not showed up at work and notified her family. Andy Lloyd, her brother, who lived in Belleville, and their mother, Roxanne McGarvey, were immediately alarmed by this and knew something bad must have happened. "It drew a red flag so quick," Andy said. "It just wasn't like her." The two rushed to her house to see what had happened. On arrival, they found her purse, wallet, and glasses inside, along with her identification. Her car remained in the driveway, but Lloyd herself was missing. One person who helped in the search noticed footprints outside her bedroom window.

Footprints that didn't belong to Lloyd.

The Belleville police were notified of her disappearance within 24 hours, and ground and aerial searches began to unfold over the weekend. They were joined by neighboring Stirling-Rawdon police department and the CFB Trenton military base. Cops and over 150 civilians volunteered to collect tips from neighboring residences. The Lloyd family, friends, and hundreds of people from nearby communities met at the local Tim Horton's coffee shop to hand out missing persons posters, which they hoped would help solve the case. The days went by with no sign of Jessica.

MURDER OF JESSICA LLOYD | 57

| Missing Person Poster of Jessica Lloyd

Warnings were sent out to nearby residents telling them to be vigilant. Women who lived alone were urged to change their routines and secure their homes. Local media in Ottawa began to report on the case, and social media became involved, with friends organizing groups on Facebook to share any updates on the case. As time passed by, the family lost hope.

Meanwhile, Williams's life resumed, the ever-professional Colonel once again taking over. He would soon be searching for another woman who would end up losing her life after a humiliating ordeal.

FUNERAL FOR JESSICA LLOYD

It was just under a week after Williams's arrest when the funeral for Jessica Lloyd was held. Over 300 people gathered to pay their final respects. Reverend Cathy Paul led the hour-long service, as well as several eulogies from close friends and relatives. John, who was Jessica's cousin, spoke for the family; her brothers and sisters were too emotional to speak.

John recalled Jessica's love for the Toronto Maple Leafs, a hockey team. "But I think God's going to have a problem with that one," he joked, hoping to lighten the somber room. "Jess was very proud of her heritage, and she was very proud of the men and women in uniform." He slowly lost control and the tears started rolling down his face. "They are strong for us every day, so at this time, I ask for friends, our family, and the whole region to be strong for them." He then thanked everyone for all the support they had offered.

Ontario Provincial Police, Belleville Police, military police, and local politicians all joined together to form an honor guard beside the funeral home as the Lloyd family left the building. Among those who were there was the mayor of Belleville, the acting commander of CFB Trenton Lieutenant Colonel David Murphy, and the chief of the Belleville Police Department. As the procession ended, bagpipers played "Amazing Grace."

WON'T YOU BE MY NEIGHBOR

Larry Jones and his wife had been living in the Cosy Cove area for over 40 years and had always loved the serenity it brought to them. Larry built his home, a red brick rancher, beside his newer neighbor, Colonel Russell Williams, about 13 years prior.

Larry was always called "Mr. Fix-it," as he would keep the neighborhood roads clean and graded, he would fix the potholes, and snowplow in winter. Larry even volunteered to build bridges and was known as the Mayor of Cosy Cove, even though they never officially had one.

It was on October 29 in the afternoon when Larry came home from hunting for partridges with his dog Wessy and noticed the police were waiting for him there.

Larry parked his Jeep and hopped out towards one of the officers who was standing in his driveway and said, "What's up, fellas? Was I robbed or something?"

It was police detective Sergeant Peter Donnelly who

responded. "I'm afraid it's a lot more serious than that, Mr. Jones." Jones immediately thought about his wife and worried that something might have happened to her, but she was at work at the time. He was about to ask if it was about her when the detective placed a stack of papers into Larry's hands and said, "You're going to have to come along with us. We can't tell you any more until we take you in for questioning. Before we take you in, we need you to unlock your door for us," Donnelly told Larry. Larry opened the door for the detective and led him into the house.

As Larry stood in his kitchen, he watched as about 20 officers came into his house, and while some started setting up an elaborate computer system in his kitchen, other officers started searching the rooms. It wasn't long before the police that were setting up their computer started to collect Jones's DVDs and CDs to scan on their computer.

Larry had recognized several of the officers, as they came from the closest detachment in Central Hastings. Detective Constable Russ Alexander seemed to be in charge; he guided Larry to his safe and asked him to open it. As Larry opened his safe, he asked the detective, "Take me in for questioning? Why is that?" Detective Donnelly firmly grabbed him by his arm and started to lead Larry to the police car and responded, "I'll tell you when you are in the car. You are not under arrest and you are free to call a lawyer."

Larry became extremely scared and could feel his heart racing; he could hardly breathe now. The detective then helped Jones into the back of the squad car and fastened the seat belt on him. As they started to pull out of the driveway, Larry noticed there were about ten officers searching his workshop, which was situated across the street from his house.

Riding to the police headquarters, all sorts of tragedies ran through his mind. Was his granddaughter okay? Did someone try and burn down his house? Were his guns stolen?

Larry then said, "Hey, I still have a shotgun in my Jeep as I just got back from my hunting trip. Make sure that you lock that up in my gun safe downstairs. I'd hate to get charged for unsafe gun storage or something like that," he said with an attitude.

Detective Donnelly, who was riding in the passenger side of the car, turned and looked at Larry and said,

"Do you realize why you're in this car?"

Larry: "No, I have no idea, I was hoping you could explain it to me."

Donnelly: "Well, we have reason to believe that you may have been involved in two sexual assaults that recently occurred on your street."

Larry moved forward in his seat and responded, "You've got to be kidding me. Are you serious?"

The car remained silent for the rest of the drive to the police detachment.

Larry Jones had been a part of the Tweed community for over 40 years now. He lived there with his wife, Bonnie, who was his high school girlfriend. They had two grown children, a son and a daughter, and five grandchildren. Both of Larry's children had built their own homes on Larry's 22-acre property so he could see his grandchildren all the time.

Larry would keep remembering how one time his daughter had come home and went into his workshop, where she surprised a tall, thin man who ran away into the woods before she could get a good look at him. Could this have been what happened? Could this man have assaulted two girls and left some evidence in his shop?

Larry had been a field manager for the Ministry of Natural Resources for ten years of his life. The government downsized the department and he was laid off. It was after his job ended with the Ministry that he became the local arena manager for the town of Tweed, where he would spend his time cleaning the ice, organizing hockey tournaments, and running the concession stand. The last job Larry had was working at the local Texaco gas station where he would tinker with mechanics on the side. It was for this reason he had built the workshop on his property.

The police took him into the interrogation room, which was only about 10' x 10' in size, with whitewashed walls and a beige laminated style flooring. Larry noticed that the room was very hot and hard to breathe in. The officer sat him on a chair and left the room. He sat slumped over at a table with his arms barely holding him up, and he looked over the room until he spotted a camera which was located in the upper right corner of the room.

Detective Donnelly entered into the room and sat in the

empty chair beside Larry. Donnelly looked sharply into Larry's eyes and started to act like they were buddies just going for a drink after a fishing trip. Larry wasn't going to have any of that. He had been around the block and understood exactly what the detective was trying to do.

Finally, after several minutes of not being able to break the ice with Larry, the detective decided to take a tougher approach.

Donnelly: "We have some tough questions for you today, Mr. Jones."

Larry looked up at Donnelly with a very stern look across his face and answered, "That's fine. I haven't done anything wrong. I've got nothing to hide. So, shoot."

Donnelly: "You, of course, have the right to counsel; would you like to call a lawyer?"

Larry: "I don't need a lawyer. I'm not guilty of any crime and you won't find anything in my house or in my truck."

Donnelly: "Is there any reason that we would have found your DNA in either of the houses of the two victims?"

Larry: "Absolutely not!" Larry then slapped both his hands onto the table with his palms facing downward. "I'll give you my DNA and my fingerprints, whatever you need to clear my name. Let's get at it!" Donnelly sat back in his chair with a startled look on his face.

Larry: "I'm not the guy, and you had better start looking in a different direction because you're barking up the wrong tree here, Mister." In the back of Larry's mind was the thought of the police focusing on him for such an awful crime, and how they were wasting their time.

Larry was also concerned about what it was that would make the police think that it was him that committed these assaults. After all, he wasn't even close to the description that the victims had given of their attacker.

The rapist was described as 30-50 years old, tall, thin, and not much hair on his body. Larry was 65 years old, 5' 11" and 215 pounds. He also had a mustache, glasses, potbelly, and lots of hair on his body. When the detective asked him to lift his shirt so they could see what his body looked like, he said, "I'm as hairy as they come." Then Larry exposed his chest and stomach to them and continued, "Do I look like your man? Do I? I've got a belly, for crying out loud. So what are you looking at me for?"

Donnelly: "We've got a pretty good lead, sir, and we have to follow it up." He let Larry sit back down in the chair, leaving his shirt untucked. "Now, if you were the man who had been in Laurie Massicotte's house and sexually assaulted her back on September 30, would you be guilty?"

Larry then blurted out a loud "No!"

Donnelly: "What do you mean? You wouldn't be guilty?"

Larry: "Of course not, because I wasn't there!"

Donnelly: "Let me ask you one more time. If you were the man who had been in Laurie Massicotte's house and sexually assaulted her back on September 30, would you be guilty?"

Larry: "The answer is the same! I'm not guilty! You can't put me in any hypothetical situation. I'm not saying I'm guilty of anything because I'm not. I'm totally innocent!"

Donnelly: "Well, you know what? A 12year-old kid could answer this question."

Larry: "Well, I'm not 12 years old."

Donnelly: "If you have skeletons in your closet, sir, now is the time to admit to them. Because we will dig them up."

Larry: "Well, go ahead, Mister, because I've only had one speeding ticket in my life."

Larry sat back into his chair now and looked up towards the camera in the room. He closed his eyes and started to think about what had just happened to him. Life was going along normally like it always had, then he comes back from his hunting trip and all of a sudden he's being interrogated by police?! His house and workshop were being taken apart and scrutinized at this very moment.

Donnelly: "So when you were growing up, what kind of relationship did you have with your father?" Larry never answered.

"Did you like your mother? Did your mother ever touch you inappropriately?" Larry continued to look towards the ceiling and say nothing.

"What kind of sex do you like? Do you like 'doggy-style'?"

It seemed like the detective was just trying to break Jones, or make him go off on a rant and perhaps catch him saying something by mistake.

Donnelly: "There are only two kinds of sex that are acceptable in society, you know?"

Jones: "And what are they?"

Donnelly: "Man on top, woman on bottom. Woman on top, man on bottom."

Larry let out a huge smile and said, "I don't know where you got this information, but it's absolutely far from the truth."

Donnelly: "Have you ever peeped in any of your neighbors' windows?"

Larry: "Never in my life."

Donnelly: "How did you get into the women's homes?"

Larry: "I didn't."

Donnelly: "Did you have the keys to these women's homes? How did you get the keys?"

Larry: "I never had keys!"

Donnelly: "How did you know that these women were alone in their home?"

Larry: "I didn't!"

Donnelly: "I hear that you are quite a pro with computers, is that correct?"

Larry: "I know how to download my camera onto the computer, and then take the computer and print a picture if

I need to, that's about it. That's all I can do. In fact, I don't even have the internet at home, and even my wife had to send and receive all of her emails from her work. Do you know that I can't even type on a computer very well?"

Donnelly got back into his chair and got really quiet. A few minutes later Larry asked, "Why do you think it's me that did this?"

Donnelly: "One of the victims, Laurie Massicotte, had recognized the voice of her attacker as you. As Larry Jones."

Larry: "That's ridiculous. Laurie and me haven't always seen eye to eye, and we live different lifestyles, but I'd never do anything to hurt her."

Donnelly asked questions for a total of three hours before asking Jones if he would take a polygraph test, which he agreed to. The local detachment did not have a polygraph machine, so they booked Jones in for a test in a week so that the police could procure a machine.

Jones was then free to go home.

When Larry Jones arrived back at his home, he went through all of his firearms to make sure every one of them was there. He was surprised, as he thought that if he was a suspect in sexual assaults, they would have confiscated his weapons.

In his kitchen was a copy of the search warrant that had been left behind by the police. When he read through the warrant, he realized that not only were the police looking for things like computers, data storage devices, cameras, and any other type of photographic equipment, but they were also on the hunt for pornographic photos and videos, and any other pornographic material of any kind. They were also searching for knives and women's clothing. The women's clothing was listed in detail by brands, sizes, designs, and color.

Larry then created a detailed list of all the items that were taken from his home by the detectives. The list consisted of his desktop computer, a laptop, two cordless mice, a Leatherman knife that was left in his Jeep, several DVDs and CDs, and his box of Playboy magazines that were hidden in his workshop.

The next day, the police called Bonnie, Larry Jones's wife, at her job to ask her to leave her work early so that she could come home and open up some safes for them. His wife and both of their kids were in shock from what had transpired, and they knew Larry all too well to even question his innocence.

A week later, Jones showed up for his appointment at the police detachment to take his polygraph test. He had been desperate to get the test done so that he could prove it wasn't him who sexually assaulted those women.

The town had been full of gossip because Larry had become the prime suspect, which had changed how Larry was being treated by his neighbors. Several people outright shunned him; others would pretend not to see him when out shopping, or even cross to the other side of the road when they saw him coming. Every time Larry went into a store, the whole room would go quiet and nobody would talk to him. If someone did talk to Larry, it would be very formal and they would act like they never knew who he was. According to Larry, whenever he was driving through town, he would notice people were always pointing at him and talking.

The officer who would be administering the polygraph test was Inspector Scott Young. He was Scottish, known to be quite brash, and a very serious man. He was short, heavy-set, and wore glasses with very thick lenses. The polygraph machine was set up in the same room that he had been interrogated in the prior week.

Larry sat in the chair and waited, saying nothing, just looking at the machine and all of the wires that came out of it.

The examiner hooked up several wires and cables to Larry, not saying a word. It would be about 15 minutes before he finished setting up, then the examiner sat in the chair beside Larry and cleared his throat.

The examiner started with all of the questions that you would expect, like how old he was, how long he had been married, how long he lived in his current house. To Larry, it seemed that the examiner would always let out a groan and roll his eyes every time Larry gave an answer.

Examiner: "Did you ever have sexual relations with Laurie Massicotte?"

Larry: "No."

Examiner: "Have you ever kissed Laurie Massicotte?"

Larry: "Yes, I did. It was at our Christmas party at our home. I kissed her as a greeting, in a nonsexual way."

The test went on for two hours before it finished. After the test was over, the examiner left the room. It was another hour before Donnelly came back into the room.

Donnelly: "Larry, you've been cleared. I was pretty certain it wasn't you, but now we know 100 percent. You go home, put your feet up, and have a cold beer. Here's my card and my number. You can contact me any time if you come up with any information, because we're really desperate for a lead on this thing."

Larry ended up going home and having about twenty of his closest friends over, and they celebrated his release from being a suspect for sexual attacks on two women.

The next thing Larry had to find out was whether Laurie Massicotte had really identified his voice as that of her rapist. Larry went to Laurie's house and asked her directly. When Laurie opened her door, she was already crying. She told him how sorry she was and that it wasn't her fault, that she had been put up to it.

Laurie would then explain how a longtime enemy of Larry's, the father of his son's ex-wife, came to her house and convinced her that the voice she heard during her attack was that of Jones. The two of them called the police and told them that Jones had the same voice as her attacker did, and the police took it from there.

Laurie couldn't explain why she went along with the plan.

She was scared and wanted to find some answers, so she just did it. Laurie asked for Larry to forgive her, but he wouldn't answer her. He just hugged her and left.

After the visit with Laurie, Jones went home, picked up Detective Donnelly's card and called him to let the detective know what he had learned. Even with this new-found information, the OPP detectives Russ Alexander and Sergeant Peter Valiquette were convinced that Jones was involved in the crimes.

For weeks and even months, the OPP would keep calling Larry's friends in for questioning about Larry's behaviors and activities. There was even a time when Larry's dirty work jacket, gloves, and a cigarette lighter went missing from his work shop. Both Larry and his wife became worried that the police were out to frame Larry.

When Bonnie went by the police detachment to pick up some of the items that had been seized during the search of their house, she confronted Detective Alexander as to why he was still investigating her husband. Alexander just denied that they were still investigating Jones and had not heard anything about it.

OBJECTS MAY APPEAR CLOSER THAN THEY ARE

"You didn't have the advantage of being able to interview the victim." – Danny Pino

After 27-year-old Jessica Lloyd went missing on January 28, 2010, police had received tips from three motorists, all recalling a vehicle parked in the field by Jessica's house on the night of her disappearance.

Investigators soon narrowed down the possible vehicles that could have left those tire track impressions.

Police then analyzed the footwear impressions that were left near the tire tracks in the field and Jessica's backyard. The tread pattern for the smaller set of prints was a match for Jessica's brown suede shoes. Based on these discoveries, police decided to set up a road block to look for any vehicles that matched the specific tires that had been identified.

On Thursday, February 4, exactly one week after Lloyd had disappeared, the Ontario Provincial Police set up a road block on Highway 37. They hoped to find something to do with the case, perhaps even come across their yet unknown suspect. They canvassed all the motorists using the highway near the missing woman's home between 7 p.m. and 6 a.m., paying attention to tire treads, one of the very few pieces of evidence that they had of the possible suspect.

Williams would drive this route normally from work every day, only instead of driving his usual BMW, he had been driving his Pathfinder, the same vehicle he had used to commit the crime. The officer that stopped Williams was initially impressed with him being a Colonel and commander of the Air Force Base in Trenton. He collected Williams's information and asked him if he knew Jessica Lloyd. Williams replied that he didn't know Miss Lloyd and hadn't seen anything unusual on his drives by her house. The officer then with a short wave said, "Thank you, sir, goodnight!" and sent Williams on his way. As he drove away, the officer's partner noticed that the tires were a match for what they were looking for.

Of course, the match by itself wasn't enough to stop him at the time, just a lead that they would make a report on. Williams probably drove away quite relieved, believing that he had gotten away with his crimes again. Little did he know that he was now under police surveillance. As investigators thought more about Williams and the proximity of the Colonel's residence to all the sexual assaults, as well as being Marie-France's commanding officer and the tire match, it was time to bring Williams in for an interview.

On Sunday, February 7, just before 2 p.m., Williams received a call at his Ottawa residence from Sergeant Jim Smyth of the OPP requesting that he come in for questioning. Williams simply accepted and went to the Ottawa police headquarters that day, not even requesting a lawyer. We still don't know why he would have gone to police headquarters to be interviewed without any counsel. Perhaps being a military officer, he was not afraid to go head to head with a police detective? Maybe he thought that the interrogation would be a simple, harmless procedure done on all the motorists that had been stopped at the road block. Perhaps he thought he could just talk himself out of any trouble if it arose. However, what followed would be the turning point in the case that led to Colonel Russell Williams finally being caught.

On February 7, 2010, Williams was interrogated at Ottawa Provincial Police headquarters by Detective Staff Sergeant Jim Smyth. The interview started at 3 p.m., and by 7:45 p.m., he was describing his crimes.

The interrogation lasted approximately ten hours.

Williams entered the room with a lot of confidence, even chewing gum, seeming quite relaxed. He threw his jacket over the back of the chair and took a seat. He took off his gloves and put them onto the desk that was in front of him. "I'm going to move your gloves," said Detective Smyth. "As you can see here, everything is being videotaped and audio taped."

"Check," Williams arrogantly responded.

INTERROGATION OF RUSSELL WILLIAMS

On Sunday, February 7, 2010, at 3:03 p.m., interrogation room 216 became the setting of one of the most intense serial killer interviews ever done in Canada. The polite, well-mannered detective opened the door to the interview room and held the door open to let in his suspect, Colonel Russell Williams.

Detective: "Just have a seat there, Russell." Williams removed his jacket and threw it over the back side of the chair the detective was pointing to.

Williams: "The guy I was speaking with the other night was Russ as well."

Detective: "Oh, yeah?"

Williams: "Yeah, he took every number that I had."

Detective: "Yeah, they were doing a pretty thorough interview that night."

Williams then pulled the chair out from under the desk in the room and took a seat.

Williams: "Absolutely. I was glad to see it." The detective then took his seat beside Williams just to his left and faced him directly.

Detective: "I'm just going to move your gloves here, that's a little microphone here."

The detective held the microphone up and showed it to Williams, then continued, "As you can see, the whole room is being recorded by video."

Williams: "Check."

Detective: "Have you ever been interviewed by the police in a room like this before?"

Williams: "I have never been in an interview like this." Williams had a grin on his face, chewing his gum with enthusiasm, and he looked up into the camera over his head for a moment.

Detective: "No? Okay." He fiddled with the microphone.

Williams: "I guess the closest to an interview like now was when I was applying for top secret clearance."

Detective: "Oh, yeah. Again, Russell, I appreciate you coming in. An investigation like this, I'm sure you can appreciate it's been big news, especially down Belleville way," Williams nodded his head yes while still chewing his gum. "And obviously, our approach to big cases like this is that we don't give up on somebody being alive until we get evidence that they're not."

Williams continued to nod his head in an up and down motion and focused on the detective's every word.

Detective: "Because of that, we're treating Jessica's as an emergency situation, so we're fast forwarding things that we might normally take our time with. That's why we're here on a Sunday afternoon. So again, I appreciate it."

Williams let out an "uh-huh."

Detective: "We're going to do a pretty thorough interview today, okay? The reason for that is because the last thing we want is to be calling people back again and again and again."

Williams: "Okay."

Detective: "So what we're going to do is go over a number of things. I'm going to explain what all of those are to you."

Williams: "Okay."

Detective: "I'm a big coffee guy. I don't know whether you're a coffee guy or not; there's some right in front of you."

Williams: "I am a coffee guy, I appreciate that! I do it black." Then Williams began mumbling.

Detective: "What was that?"

Williams: "Oh, I have a piece of gum..."

Detective: "Well, there's napkins there if you want to toss it."

Williams blushed, smiled, but kept the gum in his mouth and kept chewing. "I appreciate that."

Detective: "All right. And again, this interview is going to be very thorough, but again, I have a simple rule when I talk to people. I'm sure you're the same way. When I talk to people, I treat everyone with respect, and I expect them to do the same for me."

Williams was back to nodding his head yes and saying nothing.

Detective: "So what we're going to do is start off by going through what your rights are, okay?"

Williams: "Okay."

Detective: "Just like everybody else, okay?"

Williams: "Yeah."

Detective: "Have you ever been read your rights before?"

Williams: "No."

Detective: "I'm sure you've seen it on TV a whole bunch of times. The American version. So I'll go right ahead and read it to you briefly, okay?"

Williams: "Okay."

Detective: "Basically, in Canada, as you know, I'm sure, we all have our rights guaranteed under the Charter of Rights and Freedoms, okay?"

Williams: "Yeah, okay."

Detective: "Russell, just to avoid any confusion, and people do get confused when they talk to the police, you're obviously not under arrest here today."

Williams: "Okay."

Detective: "Anytime you feel you want to leave here, feel free to do so; the door's not locked." The detective pointed toward the door behind him and continued. "Theresa will walk you down the hallway anytime, okay?"

Williams: "Okay." He agreed, this time with a large smile across his face.

Detective: "If there's anything that comes up in our interview today, Russell, that you feel you want to talk to a lawyer about, you just let me know."

Williams: "Sure."

Detective: "And the reason I say that is I want to explain exactly what's going on here today, okay? Now, Jessica Lloyd is one of four cases that we're currently investigating. And essentially what's happened is over the past about four or five months —"

Williams: "Yeah,"

Detective: "— there have been four occurrences, like I said, that we have been looking into. Two of those occurrences happened in September 2009, and very briefly, they were up in the Tweed area. They involved somebody entering two different women's houses in the evening hours and committing a sexual act, okay?"

Williams "Yeah."

Detective: "And in November of 2009, a lady by the name of Marie-France Comeau was found murdered in her home in Brighton."

Williams: "She was one of my people."

Detective: "We believe there was a sexual component to that crime as well. And then most recently, we had Jessica Lloyd's disappearance. So essentially when we're looking at those types of crimes, we're looking at a number of potential different charges. We're looking at issues all the way from first-degree murder to kidnapping, sexual assault, break and enter with intent to commit sexual assault, forcible confinement, okay? So what I want to make sure you understand is that what we've been doing with everybody we've been talking to is that clearly when we find out who is responsible for one or all of those crimes, they could be charged with one or all of those crimes, okay? So whether it's you or anybody else."

Williams: "All right."

Detective: "That's why it's important people understand what they have to do or don't have to do when they talk with us, okay?"

Williams: "Mmm hmmm."

Detective: "So like I said before, if there's any time in the day that you feel you need to speak to a lawyer, you let me know, and we can take you to a room where you can do that in private, okay?"

Williams: "Okay."

Detective: "Do you have your own lawyer?"

Williams: "I have a realty lawyer; no, I don't have a lawyer," he said half smiling.

Detective: "All right, if at a point you want to make a call, and you don't know who to call, we have a phone list of lawyers available to give you advice, free of charge, right over the phone, okay?"

Williams: "Yep."

Detective: "So at any point you want to take advantage of that, you just let me know."

Williams: "Sure."

Detective: "Is there any reason you want to call a lawyer now?"

Williams: "Nope."

Detective: "Okay, a couple of other fairly straightforward and simple things that you probably understand. We'll go over them as well. One of those things is that you don't have to speak to me today, okay?"

Williams: "Okay."

Detective: "The reason for that is the law considers me to be a person of authority. Probably similar to what you'd be considered on the base."

Williams: "Yeah."

Detective: "And because of that, I can be compelled to speak before any judge in the country to account for what basically takes place here today between you and I, okay? And that's the reason we're being recorded here today."

Williams: "Okay."

Detective: "Because there can't be any more record than that, right?"

Williams: "Nope, understood." He still had a large grin on his face.

Detective: "And the other thing that I want to make sure that you understand is you mentioned a second ago about Miss Comeau being one of your work associates. So I don't know what's happened since November on the military side of things, but what we want to make people clear on is that if you have been spoken to by any person of authority or police officer on any of those cases, I don't want what they may have said to you make you feel influenced or compelled to say anything to me today, okay? Whatever you might have felt influenced or compelled to say to them earlier, you don't have to repeat it to me, you don't have to say anything further. But obviously what you do say, for the third time, is being recorded, okay?" The detective let out a large sigh and smiled.

Williams: "Yep, it's understood. These first two attacks that happened not that far from my place in 2009, according to you, we didn't even know the first one happened. I understand that one was reasonably close. The second one was really close."

Detective: "Yeah, I'm aware of that from looking at the different cases. And essentially, Russell, in a nutshell that's what we wanted to talk to you about. These four cases are of concern to us. And you've almost hit the nail on the head of what some of our issues are that kind of make us want to talk with Russell Williams, okay?"

Williams: "Yes."

Detective: "Because essentially there's a connection between you and all four of those cases. Would you agree?"

Williams then wildly shook his head in the yes and no directions and finally said "Geographically yes. I drive past, yes, I would say there's a connection."

Detective: "Yeah, yeah, and that's why, I'll be quite frank with you, that's why things kind of evolved with you, when the officers talked with you on Thursday night." This was during the road block the police set up to look for a certain type of vehicle and tread that left impressions on the ground at the scene.

Williams: "Okay."

Detective: "It kind of went from there, because I think that you discussed with them that you're a Colonel at the base —"

Williams interrupted "I was in a uniform at the time, so..."

Detective: "— yeah, so it was pretty obvious."

Williams: "Yep."

Detective: "Yeah, so essentially the connection with Miss Comeau was made. And I believe that you're a door or two down from one of those incidents in Tweed."

Williams: "Yeah, three doors down, very close essentially."

Detective: "Exactly, so those are some of the issues we want to discuss with you."

Williams: "Yeah, okay."

Detective: "So just getting back to these four incidents that we were talking about, maybe you can just give me a little bit of history of your arrival in the base in Trenton. When did you start working there?"

Williams: "Friday in the day. I was..." Williams then looked down towards his left and continued to chew his gum and paused for a minute. "Friday in the day, I was home most of the time." Then he looked up and into the face of the detective and continued. "Friday in the day I was home. I had a sort of stomach flu."

Detective: "Okay, in Ottawa or Tweed?"

Williams: "In Tweed."

Detective: "In Tweed, Okay. So to back track then, so all day Friday you were home?"

Williams: "Yep."

Detective: "And then what time did you leave to the base to sleep there Friday night?"

Williams: "Um, I'm not sure." He paused for another minute slightly shaking his head back and forth, then continued. "I'm not sure. I probably went in just before bed, so probably between 8 and 9 or something."

Detective: "Okay. And you get to the base and spend the evening there, and for the 5:30 —"

Williams cuts in again. "Yep."

Detective: "Okay. So when we back track from there, you arrived home at your cottage, I don't want to get confused between your home in Ottawa and your cottage in Tweed, so…"

Williams: "Yeah, I had been in Tweed all week. The week prior now." He took another long pause, this time looking up to his left. "Yep, that's the case all week, flu Saturday, and went to Ottawa Saturday night." He then looked back at the detective, nodding his head yes.

Detective: "Okay, so if you didn't have the stomach flu on the Friday, what was your schedule that day?"

Williams continued to chew his gum and let out a low moan, and took another minute to answer. "What would have been my schedule? Oh, just a standard schedule in the office."

Detective: "Okay."

Williams: "So, uh, brief in the morning, a couple of meetings." Another long pause as if he was thinking hard to remember. "I can't remember the specifics we were in."

Detective: "Okay, so Thursday night you slept at Tweed, or …?"

Williams: "Yep."

Detective: "All right, and what did you do on Thursday in the day?"

Williams: "Thursday during the day, I was at the base again." He got quiet and let out another slight moan, and started to shake his head no. "I think it was a normal day, I can't recall exactly. Yeah, nothing out of sorts, so I was at the base all day. I would have gone in early in the morning, back home in the evening."

Detective: "Okay, do you remember what time you left the base that night?"

Williams again looked to his left and was now chewing his gum slowly, keeping his mouth closed, and after a solid minute spoke again.

Williams: "I don't remember anything peculiar, so I would say I was there probably between 7 and 9, somewhere in that range."

Detective: "Okay, and that's when you left?"

Williams: "Yes that's when I left, yeah, about 45 minutes home."

Detective: "About a 45-minute transit?"

Williams: "Yeah."

Detective: "Now, I'm not going to walk you through November, but I'm going to take you to a date that's probably pretty fresh in your mind. The day that Marie-France Comeau —"

Williams interrupted. "Yep."

Detective: "Do you remember how you found out?"

Williams: "I do, yeah. I was sent an email...um..." Another

long pause with a deep breath in and out. "Well, as soon as the ops staff in the base learned, they told me."

Detective: "Okay."

Williams: "So I got an email in, I can't remember if it was late at night or early in the morning. It was certainly...I saw it, I want to say, first thing in the morning, because I just got back from Ottawa. I was in Ottawa for a set of meetings, I don't know what days of the week we're talking about. But, uh, yeah, no, I mean once you learn one of your people gets killed, you know, it gets your attention."

Detective: "Absolutely."

Williams: "I very much remember that time."

Detective: "And how did you know Marie-France Comeau?"

Williams: "I only met her once. Um, she was on a crew I was on just after I got to the base."

Detective: "Okay."

Williams: "So I can't even remember, I think it was a one-day trip. I did one of our trips in Canada transporting out troops for the first leg, out of Edmonton. We tend to hopscotch them across until they get into theater, so. Anyway, I can't remember what it was, but we did a number to Edmonton, just to pick up the troops and then, um, put a fresh crew on. Because we fly them back to the same destination."

Detective: "Okay. Do you know roughly when that happened?"

Williams: "That we were on the same crew?"

Detective: "The time you had, the one time with her, yeah."

Williams: "It was after I got to the base, so it was, you know, I don't remember exactly, but I would say that it was in the first couple of months, so August/September."

Detective: "Okay. Now you got that email to notify you that something had happened. Do you have a clear recollection of how your schedule was going that week?"

Williams would make the same turn of his head, up and to the left, away from the face of the detective, and he would breathe in heavy and release it with another sigh.

Williams: "I don't remember again what day that the message came in. Just a second." Another long pause went by before he said, "No, no, I can't remember what day that was, but I, there was a whole bunch of activity spun up because of it, I can tell you." Another long pause. "No, I can't remember the day of the week. I'm trying to remember what reports I had going that week...no, I can't remember, I'm sorry. What we learned after the fact was that the MPs had learned of her death, I think quite a bit after her body had been discovered." Williams looked directly into the detective's eyes as if he expected the detective to give him the answer. Instead, the detective just said okay.

Williams continued after another long pause. "I think what happened was the MPs learned late that evening, I can't remember when. Obviously her body was discovered, it was probably in the news reports. But they learned, then they passed it to ops, and so they immediately passed it to me. Along with some others."

Detective: "Right. When you got the email, do you remember where you were?"

Williams: "I was at home in Tweed."

Detective: "Do you remember if that was a week that you were in Trenton, or had you flown?"

Williams: "No, I had been in Ottawa early in the week for some meeting over in Gatineau for an acquisition, so I had been here, but I can't remember how the days all fell together. I seem to remember having got this word shortly after I got back from Ottawa. Seems to me it was the same week."

Detective: "So if we were to do a similar investigation into your background, is there anything that anybody may have misinterpreted, or is there anything in your history that somebody might say that Russell Williams did this?"

Williams: "No. It'll be very boring."

The detective let out a laugh and said "Because essentially, that's what I'm looking at. You seem like a very intelligent person, and you can certainly see how a surprise like that would..."

Williams: "Absolutely."

Detective: "So the next thing we need to cover off, okay, I'll just ask you this straight out. Given the types of crimes that we're investigating, do you get much chance to watch television shows like CSI?"

Williams: "I do, yeah. I prefer Law and Order, but I do watch CSI occasionally, yes."

Detective: "Okay, so you have an idea of the forensic capabilities and things like that out there?"

Williams: "Yes."

Detective: "What would you be willing to give me today to move past you in this investigation?"

Williams: "What, uh, what do you need?"

Detective: "Would you be willing to supply things like fingerprints, blood samples, things like that?"

Williams: "Sure."

Detective: "Right, footwear impressions?"

Williams: "Right."

Detective: "I think that's what we're going to ask you to do. Now, we have a process that we have to go through in order for you to do that."

Williams: "Okay."

Detective: "And for the blood sample, I don't take blood samples. We have specially trained officers to do that. I'm going to step out and make sure they're still available."

Williams: "Okay."

BLOOD TEST BREAK

A few minutes later, an officer came into the interview room and took Williams to a small makeshift medical room. There, a nurse came in and took Williams's blood for testing. After the tests were completed, the officer returned Williams to the interrogation room. As soon as Williams got back to the room, he took a seat, crossed his arms, and let out a sigh. Detective Smyth came back into the room and took a seat beside Williams at the table. The detective opened up his binder and started to shuffle through the papers that were inside of it.

Williams: "Can I assume you're going to be discreet?"

Detective: "It's possible, yep."

Williams: "Because you know, this can have a very significant...on the base, if they thought that you guys thought I did this."

Detective: "Well, Russell, that's one of the reasons we're here on a Sunday afternoon. The military would certainly be a great assistance to us, especially in relation to Miss Comeau's investigation, so this was certainly one of the reasons we called you on a Sunday to see if you could sit with us today."

Williams: "Okay. Cause it's tough to undo the rumor mill once it gets started."

There was a knock at the door and the detective got up to see who it was. When he opened the door, there was two detectives standing there. They had a few brief words, and then Detective Smyth turned around and asked Williams if he could remove his shoes.

Williams, who was still seated, agreed and removed his shoes. Detective Smyth picked them up and gave both shoes to the detectives at the door. He turned around and told Williams he'd just be a minute.

SHOE SAMPLE BREAK

Detective: "Now that you've had some time to think about things, I know we've thrown a lot at you here, are you concerned about that swab matching at any of those four residences?"

Williams: "No."

Detective: "Let me explain what I'm getting at here, Russell. This is a significant investigation, as you can well imagine, and DNA is going to be significant in our investigation. Both quite possibly to help you and quite possibly to help us. I don't know yet, I don't know the results yet. I'll go back to the example I gave you, a very similar issue that I think you talked about. You talked about the idea of unusual sex acts, or extra-marital affairs or indiscretions, things along those lines. Is there any contact you may have had with any of those four women that you may not want your wife to be aware of, anything like that, that we should be aware of? To try and explain why, if your DNA is found, to help us understand why it may be there?"

Williams: "Absolutely not." His arms were crossed now and he steadily shook his head no.

Detective: "Can you think of any reason why there might be your DNA in any of those residences?"

Williams: "No."

Detective: "Let's focus on the house just a couple doors down from you in Tweed there."

Williams: "A couple doors down was Laurie, I don't know her last name."

Detective: "Massicotte?"

Williams: "I don't even know what her last name is, but the woman down the road, three doors down, her name is Laurie, I don't know her last name."

Detective: "Let me make sure we're on the same page here." The detective went through his book of notes, then continued. "My understanding is she lived at 76 Cosy Cove, yes, so she would be the one, the second one that, the second incident on your road there."

Williams: "Yep, a couple doors down."

Detective: "Have you ever been to her house?"

Williams took another long pause, again staring to the left of him at the wall, still with his arms crossed.

Williams: "No. We met her once, I think, the first summer, um, we were there, so in '04."

Detective: "Okay, and that's what I'm getting at. Again, this is a credibility issue. I don't want to come to you in two or three weeks from now and say, Russ, our CSI people were in that house and...are you familiar with how DNA works?"

Williams: "I think broadly, yes, I think so."

Detective: "One of the challenges we have is that in 2010,

DNA has become so precise that...I guess the best way to explain it is this: I can think back 15 years ago when I started in violent crime investigations. For us to get a DNA match, the sample we had to find was probably what would have filled half of one of these cups." He then held his coffee cup up and looked towards it and Williams agreed. He then continued. "Because they destroy so much of the sample in the testing."

Williams: "Okay."

Detective: "Um, essentially, DNA has become more and more precise to the point where when you and I walked in this room earlier today, we could have sat down and talked for about 30 seconds and walked out, a CSI officer could have come in three or four days from now and did some swabs here, and he could have found your DNA and my DNA and probably a lot of other peoples' DNA."

Williams: "Sure."

Detective: "You know, as we talk, a little bit of aspirate comes out of our mouths."

Williams: "Sure, I understand."

Detective: "That contains our DNA. Our skin cells contain our DNA."

Williams: "Yeah."

Detective: "And that's what I'm getting at. If you were ever in Laurie's residence…"

Williams: "No."

Detective: "Quite possibly, quite innocently, your DNA

could be in that residence. So, has there ever been a time that you were in there?"

Williams: "No. No!" He said firmly, his arms still crossed.

Detective: "What about the other lady down the road?"

Williams: "No, I hadn't even heard that name, so no, I don't actually know who that was."

Detective: "Okay, have you ever visited Marie-France Comeau's residence?"

Williams: "No."

Detective: "Okay, you're positive that your DNA won't be at any of those locations?"

Williams: "No."

Detective: "Did you know Jessica Lloyd, even in passing for any reason?"

Williams: "No. I never heard her name until it was on the news."

Detective: "The reason I'm asking you is that because I know you were asked that question on Thursday night, and sometimes what we find, and again this is one of those situations that could sometimes cause us to get into a lengthy investigation of somebody that doesn't deserve it, but what can happen sometimes is somebody can get stopped by the police, like you did, and they get asked that question. And people that get stopped by the police can get nervous, so they blurt out an answer and they start driving away and say, 'Why did I do that?' because the problem is once they get asked again, they feel compelled to maintain that answer, for fear that if they change their answer, somebody could find that, do you know what I mean?"

Williams: "Yeah, yeah, I do."

Detective: "So to make sure that's not happening here, I don't care what you said to the officer on Thursday night last week. If there's any communication or contact between you and Jessica Lloyd...You've seen her picture, right?"

Williams: "Yeah, I have, absolutely."

Detective: "Ever seen her before?"

Williams: "I don't, no, I'd say I have not."

Detective: "You mentioned something about doing some renovations at your property in Tweed there. I think you said something about tearing up your carpet there?"

Williams: "Yeah."

Detective: "When did all of that happen?"

Williams: "In 2004 or 2005."

Detective: "Okay. Any recent renovations?"

Williams: "Nope."

Detective: "All right." The detective then started to look through his notepad. "I just want to make sure I'm covering all the bases here." After a long pause and searching through his papers he asked, "What kind of tires do you have on your Pathfinder?"

Williams: "I think, I think they're Toyo."

Detective: "Do you know a brand name or the make?"

Williams: "Sorry, I don't remember, the make is Toyo, I don't know the model."

Detective: "Okay, I'm just going to read this off to you and see if it rings a bell." He flipped through some more of his papers. "Ever hear of, or does Toyo Open Country HTS sound familiar?"

Williams: "Yes, that's it."

Detective: "When did you have those tires put on your Pathfinder?"

Williams: "Well, it's the second version that we had of them, so I think it might have been this past fall. They replaced the other ones that we had on. I can't say that they were the same, exactly the same model, but our dealership here in Ottawa say they're very popular for the Pathfinders. They were good, they lasted a long time."

Detective: "All right, um, you were talking about the whole idea of the MPs helping us with our investigation. You have the same system as we do at our headquarters, of course, with the swipe cards."

Williams: "Yes."

Detective: "One of the things is, one of our investigators made a call while I was talking to you there, because we were trying to work through that week of November 23..."

Williams: "Okay."

Detective: "The 23rd being a Monday, and the 24th being a Tuesday."

Williams: "Okay."

Detective: "What they told us is, I want to make sure I get this right..." Then he paused again to look over his papers. "Is that on the 23rd, your swipe card was being used at the base, and Tuesday the 24th, there was no use of the card."

Williams: "Okay."

Detective: "Then on the following days, the Wednesday, Thursday, and Friday, there was what appeared to be average activity of your swipe card at the base. Does that make sense to you?"

Williams: "It does. It says that I was in Ottawa on the Tuesday."

Detective: "Do you remember where in Ottawa that you were?"

Williams: "Yes. I was in Gatineau, like I said, with a meeting about the C-17."

Detective: "Okay. Again, I want to be fair to you. We're going back two months...are you sure that would have been the day you were in Ottawa?"

Williams: "Well, only because I wasn't at the base. So, I can't remember honestly if that's the day I had to be in Ottawa, but if I wasn't at the base, it's because I was here."

Detective: "Okay then, if that is the day that you had a meeting in Ottawa, do you remember being at the base on the Monday, the 23rd, and swiping your card in and out? Do you remember what you would have done that evening to get to Ottawa for that meeting?"

Williams: "I drove to Ottawa in the morning of the day of my meeting, so if it was Tuesday, I would have left Tweed, it was a very foggy morning that morning."

Detective: "Okay."

Williams: "And I drove in that morning." Williams then shrugged his shoulders with his arms still being crossed. "So, I would not have been at the base the day I was in Ottawa, because the meeting started at 8:30 or something."

Detective: "Okay, so you leave the base, you would have gone home to your residence in Tweed, and then you left Tweed in the morning, and drove up to your meeting in Ottawa?"

Williams: "Yep."

Detective: "You leave the meeting in Ottawa, was it a daytime meeting or evening meeting, do you remember?"

Williams: "Yep, yeah, it was a daytime meeting. It finished mid afternoon or something. We had lunch and we finished. I think my wife and I had dinner because she was here for work, and then I headed back."

Detective: "Okay, these are the kinds of things I'm trying to draw out here. It's helpful to us. Do you remember where you had dinner?"

Williams started to laugh. "I don't remember where we had dinner, but it was in Westboro because that's where our house was being built at the time, so we had dinner, you know, in a restaurant that we would expect to be able to frequent once the house was finished."

Detective: "Okay, do you remember how you paid?"

Williams: "One of us would have paid by MasterCard."

Detective: "Okay, are you sure about that?"

Williams: "Pretty sure, that's normally how we pay for meals. I can't remember if it was me or my wife who paid, but it was one of us."

Detective: "Okay, and you can't remember which restaurant it was again? You see what I'm getting at, right? That could be very helpful to us if we could track that issue, right?"

Williams: "Right."

Detective: "We could put somebody paying for a meal at a location."

Williams: "I mean, I was eating with 15 people or so that day, you know."

Detective: "What time did that meeting end?"

Williams let out a big sigh and said, "I would say between 3 and 4."

Detective: "Okay, and, um, are you sure that's the same day you went out with your wife?"

Williams: "Well, I think so because she was here, and I think that was the day we went to this restaurant in Westboro, yes."

Detective: "You finished dinner and you remember what you did that evening?"

Williams: "I would have driven back to Tweed."

Detective: "Okay, and you would have, I know we're talking two months ago, but do you remember having dinner and specifically driving back to Tweed or are you just guessing here?"

Williams: "No, I'm not really guessing. I mean, I believe that this night at this restaurant was following the meetings in Ottawa, and then I kissed my wife goodbye and I headed back to Tweed to go to work the next day."

Detective: "Okay. The tires that you have on your truck, the reason I asked you about that, is there any time you recall where you were stopped by the officers there?"

Williams: "Yes."

Detective: "Did they explain to you what the significance was to you there?"

Williams: "They said that was her house."

Detective: "That was her house?"

Williams: "Yes."

Detective: "So you remember that location?"

Williams: "Yep."

Detective: "Do you remember what the crossroad was?"

Williams: "I don't think there was a crossroad. It was just the south end of 37."

Detective: "Okay, when you get stopped at that location, has there been a time in the recent one or two weeks that your vehicle has left that road for any reason whatsoever? Have you driven into a field with your vehicle at all for any reason that you can think of?"

Williams: "Nope."

Detective: "So I want you to rack your brain here, this is important. Is there anything that you can remember doing that would have caused you to drive off the road at that section of roadway?"

Williams: "Nope. That's the early part of the highway, I just head north. It's about 30 minutes from there to, no probably 20, from there to my house."

Detective: "Okay. Would it surprise you to know that when the CSI officers were looking around her property, that they identified a set of tire tracks, to the north of her property, that look as if the vehicle left the road and drove along the north tree line of Jessica Lloyd's property?"

Williams: "Okay."

Detective: "They examined those tire tracks and they have contacts in the tire business. You see, tire tracks are a major source of evidence for us."

Williams: "Sure."

Detective: "Shortly after this investigation started, they identified those tires as the same tires on your Pathfinder."

Williams: "Really?!"

Detective: "Yeah."

Williams: "Okay." Again, shaking his head no.

Detective: "One of the other things that they do is to try and identify the type of vehicle that would have left those tires...Well, they do two things. They talk to witnesses. There was a female police officer who drove by that location that evening who recalls seeing an SUV-type vehicle in the field just north of Jessica Lloyd's house consistent with a Pathfinder."

Williams: "Okay."

Detective: "What they also do to try and identify the vehicle is they look at the wheel base width. Because different vehicles, different makes and models, have different wheel base width. So, they can take tire tracks and measure the distance between them, and determine what the width is, and they can enter that into a vehicle database and it will spit out the kinds of vehicles."

Williams: "Okay."

Detective: "Your Pathfinder's wheel base width is very very close to the width of the tire treads that were left in that field. Okay, do you have any recollection at all of being off that road?"

Williams: "No, I was not off that road, no."

Detective: "Okay. Russell, is there anything you can think of? Let's talk about Marie-France Comeau for a minute. Is there any reason at all that you can think of...During our investigation, we're searching computers, things like Blackberries, right, electronic devices, looking through houses for things that are in writing, notes, diaries, things like that. Now, I'm not at liberty to tell you what the content is. Is there any reason at all that you can think of for why Marie-France Comeau would have specifically referenced you in some of her writings?"

Williams: "Not at all." He took a short pause. "No, absolutely not."

Detective: "Okay, is there anything she ever said to you that led you to believe that there may be something, more than a passing interest with her towards you?"

Williams: "Not at all. No, we spent only one flight together. I'd go back and occasionally talk. No, if that's the case, that's very surprising."

Detective: "All right, do you have any questions for me right now?"

Williams: "No."

Detective: "I'm just going to step out and see how things are going. I mean, it is a Sunday, but there are probably 60 or 70 people working on this file, so there are a lot of things happening. So, let me go out and see what's going on and I'll come back in and hopefully continue."

Williams: "Okay."

William's Pathfinder tire tread matches scene of the murder

WARRANT TO SEARCH WILLIAMS'S HOUSE AND CABIN BREAK

As the detective walked back in the room with his papers shoved into a binder, held up under his right arm, he started to speak.

Detective: "Remember when we first came in here, I told you that I'm going to treat you with respect and I asked you to do the same for me?" The detective put his papers on the table, sat down, and looked directly into Williams's face. "We talked about the whole idea of how we approached you here and try to be as free as possible."

Williams: "Okay." Still with his arms crossed.

Detective: "The problem is, Russell, that every time I leave this room, there's another issue that comes up. And it's not issues that point away from you, it's issues that point at you, okay? And I want you to see what I mean."

The detective then opened his binder and started shuffling through his mess of papers, scattering them onto the table. He located one and turned to face Williams and said, "This is the footwear impression." Williams bent over in his chair to get a closer look at the paper the detective was holding out in front of him. "Of the person who approached the rear of Jessica Lloyd's house on the evenings of the 28th and 29th of January, okay? Now, I want you to keep in mind that this is slightly smaller in scale, okay?"

Williams was still bent over, and he looked up. "Okay."

Detective: "That's not to scale, okay? If you look here on

the ruler, you'll see that one inch is just slightly smaller than an inch, okay? But this is the way that it prints off on the computer." The detective put the picture back onto the table and continued. "Essentially, when you're dealing with footwear impressions...we have a gentleman on the OPP who's basically world-renowned. His name is John Norman. Essentially, with footwear impressions, you're pretty much in the area of fingerprints. What we're talking about here, especially when you start adding in other pieces of information that support an investigative position..." The detective stopped talking and reached over to his left and picked up a different piece of paper that was folded in half. He opened it up and laid it on the table in front of Williams. "This is a photocopy of the boot that we took off your foot just a little while ago."

Williams: "Yep."

Detective: "Now, I'm not an expert in footwear impressions, but I rely on the experts. Footwear impressions are very much like fingerprint comparisons. You take a look at this print, and again this is one print, there's several different prints to compare. So, we are going to get features off of one print to compare and another feature off of another print to compare."

Williams: "Yep."

The detective ran his hand over the picture and continued. "These are identical." There was a long pause in the room while Williams looked intently over the footprint picture.

Detective: "Your vehicle drove up the side of Jessica Lloyd's house, your boots walked to the back of Jessica

Lloyd's house on the evening of the 28th and 29 of January. Okay? You want discretion, we need to have some honesty, okay? Because this is getting out of control really fast, Russell, okay? Really, really fast."

Williams let out an "umm" and took hold of the footprint picture and looked it over closely, not saying a word.

Detective: "This is getting beyond my control, right? I came in here a few hours ago, and I called you in today because I wanted to give you the benefit of the doubt, but you and I both know you were at Jessica Lloyd's house, and I need to know why."

Again, there was another long silence in the room. Williams then sat up, keeping a hold of the footprint picture, which he moved over to his lap, and he continued to stare at it. As he started to shake his head to say no, he said, "I don't know what to say."

Detective: "Well, you need to explain it. This is the other problem we're having, Russell." The detective leaned over to his left again, opened up his binder and pulled out another sheet of paper. He faced back in front of Williams holding the paper with both hands over his knees. "Again, these decisions aren't made by me. Right now there's a search warrant being executed at your house." The detective then placed the warrant on the table in front of Williams.

Detective: "So, your wife now knows what's going on. Here is the search warrant for your place in Tweed, and your vehicles have been seized, okay? You and I both know what they're going to find. Evidence that's going to link you to these situations. You and I both know that the unknown offender male DNA on Corporal Marie-France Comeau's body is going to be a match to you, quite possibly before the evening is over. This is a major investigation. The Center for Forensic Sciences is on call 24 hours a day, and they're helping us with it. Your opportunity to take some control here and have some explanation that anybody is going to believe is quickly expiring."

Williams was now nodding his head yes as if agreeing with the detective. He still remained quiet. The detective continued. "The investigators now are applying for a search warrant to search your office. These aren't decisions we can say yes or no to, these are practical steps in an investigation like this."

At this time, Williams sat up with his back against the chair and let out another big sigh. He continued to look at the paper with the shoe prints on them and remained quiet for another few minutes until the detective called out his name. "Russell!" Williams looked up like a child that was caught and let out an "Uh huh?"

Detective: "Listen to me for a second, okay?"

Williams then put the shoe print picture back onto the table in front of him. The detective then took all of the papers that he had pulled out and neatly placed them into a pile. "When that evidence comes in, when the DNA is a match, when that phone rings, or somebody knocks on that door, your credibility is gone, okay? Because this is how credibility works. I know you're an intelligent guy, and you probably don't need to hear this explanation, but I also know your mind is racing right now. I've sat across from a lot of people in your position over the years. The bottom line is as soon as we get that piece of evidence that solidifies it, the DNA, as soon as the experts in footwear impressions and the expert in tire impressions calls and says, "yes, I examined those and they're a match," it's all over. Because as soon as that happens, where's your credibility? Where's your believability? You're just another, um, again don't take this wrong, but you can see if you step outside this room in your mind. And you can imagine how people are going to view you if the truth comes out after the clear evidence is presented to you. When you finally go, 'okay, I'm screwed now'."

Williams sits back in his chair again, still with his arms crossed, no longer chewing on his gum, but now looking right at the detective and slowly shaking his head in an affirmative way. There was another long pause, only to be broken by the detective. "Russell, you know there's only one option, what other option is there?"

Williams: "What's the option?"

Detective: "Well, I don't think you want the cold-blooded psychopath option." Russell let out another sigh. "I might be wrong...don't get me wrong, because I've met guys who actually kind of enjoyed the notoriety, got off on it. Got off on having that label, Bernardo being one of them. I don't see that in you. If I saw that in you, I wouldn't be back here talking to you. But maybe I'm wrong, maybe you got me fooled, you know? This is over, and it can have a bad ending where Jessica's parents continue to wonder where their daughter is lying."

Williams now seemed scared stiff, not moving at all.

Detective: "I don't know, there's a search going on and it will continue, it will continue until her body is found. That might even happen tonight for all I know. Once that happens, then I don't know what other cards you'll have to play. What are we going to do?"

Williams remained in the exact same position. You could only hear him breathing and every once in a while, sigh. He then looked down toward his left.

Detective: "Russell, what are we going to do?"

Williams finally spoke. "Call me Russ, please."

Detective answered, "Okay, what are we going to do, Russ?"

Detective: "Is Jessica somewhere we could find her easily? Is it something that I could call somebody, tell them to go to a location and find her? Or is this somewhere we would have to go and take a walk?"

Another few minutes went by and Williams sighed again.

Detective: "Which direction are we headed in here?" There was another long pause. "Russ, maybe this will help. Can you tell me what issue you're struggling with?" After another few minutes without an answer from Williams, he asked again. "What's the issue you're struggling with?"

After another long pause, Williams finally spoke, "It's hard to believe that this is happening."

Detective: "Why is that? Why is it hard to believe?"

Williams then reached over to the papers on the table. "It's just hard, it's just hard to believe."

Detective: "Whose decision was it? We're going to find out the answer to this anyway. Whose decision was it to issue the order to the base personnel that nobody had to speak to the police and to seek legal counsel before they were questioned?"

Williams looked puzzled. "I don't think that was..."

The detective broke in. "It's my understanding that was what came from somebody who reports to you."

Williams: "Well..."

Detective: "Russ, what do you think they are going to say? Let's step back for a second here, okay? I really don't think it benefits you or makes you look any better to start debating the little issues."

Williams came back aggressively. "No, no, no, that is news to me, I have a legal officer who reports to me who may have given that direction. That's the first time I have heard of it, and that's the truth. That's the first time I've heard of that."

Detective: "And that may be the case, but how does it look? We're not even dealing with something that is evidence, we don't need it. We got DNA and all this other stuff."

Williams then looked at the detective with an inquisitive look. "What was the question?"

Detective: "I can't recall, but it was something along the lines of telling the people on the base that they weren't required legally to speak with the police, and that they should seek legal counsel before they decide to speak."

Williams: "Well, if that was actually said, it would have not been to the base. It may have been to an individual, the boyfriend of the suspect."

Detective: "Okay, I understand that it went out to all personnel?"

Williams: "No."

BATHROOM BREAK

While Williams was using the bathroom, the detective got some more maps from Google and blew up their sizes and printed them off.

Williams came back into the interview room and sat in his chair with his arms crossed again.

Williams: "You talked about perception. My only two immediate concerns from a perception concern are what my wife must be going through right now, and the impact this is going to have on the Canadian Forces."

Detective: "Where do we go? Russ, is there anything you want from me? Is there anything you want me to explain? Is there something missing that you are struggling with that I could shed some light on for you?"

Williams let out another large sigh. "I'm struggling with how upset my wife is right now."

Detective: "Russ, what are you looking for?"

Williams leaned over and picked up some of the papers of evidence that the detective had in a pile on the desk and started to speak softly again, keeping his facing down, making it harder for the detective to hear him. "I'm concerned that they are tearing apart my wife's new house."

The detective quickly responded. "So am I, but if nobody tells them what's there and what's not, they don't have a choice." Williams put down the papers and sat back in his chair.

Detective: "This investigation will cost no less than 10 million dollars easy, and they will say no to nothing. Any requests that they may request on this case, they've already been told are approved, don't even bother asking. So, what am I doing here, Russ? I've put my best foot forward for you here, I really have. I don't know what else to do to make you understand the impact of what's happening here."

Williams continued to move around in his chair and sigh.

Detective: "Do we talk?"

Williams: "I want to minimize the impact on my wife."

Detective: "So do I."

Williams: "So how do we do that?"

Detective: "Well, we start by telling the truth."

Williams: "Okay."

Detective: "Okay, so, where is she?"

Williams: "You got a map?"

Detective: "Is she close to where she lives? I got a map of

that general area. Which town is she near? Why don't we start there?"

Williams: "I'm not sure if you'll need a map of...to the highway and over to Tweed and south. I'll show you."

Detective: "Let me see what I got here, I might have something." The detective then opened up his binder again and started looking through it. "Is she inside or outside?"

Williams: "Outside." It took another couple of minutes for the detective to find the map, and then he slid his chair over so that he was sitting right next to Williams.

Detective: "This is probably the biggest area I have there, Russ."

Williams: "I need more. I need a real map."

Detective: "So where am I going on here to get to her?"

Williams let out another loud sigh and pointed to a spot on the map. "In this spot here."

Detective: "Okay so you're pointing to…."

Williams: "I need a detailed map of that area to show you where she is."

Detective: "Okay, is she close to a road?"

Williams: "Yep."

Detective: "Is it something where, is she buried, or if you walk there, you would fairly easily see her?"

Williams: "It's here." He pointed toward the spot without touching the map.

Detective: "Okay, so she's south of 7, east of Tweed, west of 41, and what's this road here?"

Williams: "I'm not sure."

Detective: "Neither am I. Okay, I'll be right back. Do you want any water or anything?"

Williams: "Sure."

Detective: "Okay, I'll be right back." The detective stood up and started to gather all of his papers and put them back into his binder. "How long has she been there for?"

Williams: "A little over a week."

Detective: "Was it fairly quick from the time she left?"

Williams: "Friday night."

Detective: "Friday night?"

Williams: "Yep."

Detective: "So where was she between Thursday night and Friday night?"

Williams: "In Tweed."

Detective: "With you?"

Williams: "Yep."

Detective: "How long was she alive for?"

Williams started rocking back and forth in his chair, keeping his arms crossed. "Almost 24 hours."

Detective: "Okay, Russ." Williams looked up at the detective. "You're doing the right thing here."

Williams started to move his head in an affirmative manner, then reached out his hand, and the two men shook hands.

Williams: "Again, my interest here is making my wife's life a little bit easier here. Yeah, and her family as well."

Detective: "Well, we share that interest."

Williams: "There's no, your time in Ottawa is wasted, really. I'll tell you where the memory cards are. They are in the house there, but..."

Detective: "In Ottawa?"

Williams: "Yep."

Detective: "Where about?"

Williams: "Some in the camera bag that they would have found in my office. And then in the office, when you walk in, on the left-hand side there's a desk, a set of drawers, like a filing cabinet, wooden IKEA. In one of the top two drawers, there's a plastic divider."

Detective: "Yep."

Williams: "And there's a, inside there, there are two memory cards."

Detective: "And whose images are on those cards?"

Williams: "Well, I've erased them, but I expect that you'll be able to draw images of Jessie and I."

Detective: "What about Marie-France?"

William unexpectedly looked up and had a smirk on his

face. "There may be images on there as well."

Detective: "And the two others from September?"

Williams: "Yep."

Detective: "Do you have those images stored anywhere else?"

Williams: "Yep, there are two hard drives in the house in Ottawa. I can draw you a little picture if you like."

Detective: "Sure, do you want to do that now?"

Williams: "Sure."

The detective then found a clean piece of paper and placed it in front of Williams. "Do you want something to eat?"

Williams picked up a pen and started to draw on the paper and said no. Then he continued to draw the map and, after a few minutes, said, "But I do want to talk to you again."

Detective: "That's the plan, okay?" He then picked up his binder and said, "I'll be back." He left the room.

BREAK

While the detective was gone, Williams drew out a map to where the two hard drives that contained the images could be found in Ottawa.

The detective came back into the interview room carrying two drinks. "How you making out there?" He placed the drinks on the table in front of Williams.

Williams quickly looked up at the detective briefly and

said, "Okay."

The detective closed the door to the room and picked up some papers. "I have someone running around trying to find a map, so what I did is blow up a Google map of the area." Then he placed it down on the table in front of Williams. "This one might have better perimeters for you. Here's Tweed."

Williams moved the map and started to draw on it. He started speaking lightly, almost mumbling. "It's about 0.7 kilometers from this intersection, behind Sutton Road."

Detective: "How far off the road is she?"

Williams: "40 feet."

Detective: "Is she buried, is she covered with anything?"

Williams shook his head no and said, "She's wrapped up and she's on the surface."

Detective: "The obvious question I'm going to have there for you, when they go there, they'll be there shortly, they're going to find her?"

Williams: "Oh, yeah."

Detective: "Okay. I'll be right back. It looked like you wanted to say something?"

Williams: "Just that, this place, my wife...it's been a dream for her for the better part of a year. I'm keen to get them what they need, so they can leave her alone."

Detective: "Well, we will do our best to keep it as low key as possible."

CONFESSIONS OF A MADMAN

The detective came back into the room and sat down. "What do you want to talk about?"

Williams: "I guess it's pretty wide open now, eh?"

Detective: "Yeah."

Williams: "What do you want to know?"

Detective: "Well, do you want to work forwards or backwards?"

Williams: "Doesn't matter."

Detective: "Why don't we start with Jessica? How does that start for you?"

Williams: "I saw her in her house on her treadmill, Wednesday night I guess, and I noticed she wasn't there Thursday. So I got in the house and looked around, then I left. I noticed she came home, so I went back in through the back patio door while she was sleeping." Williams took a long pause.

Detective: "Okay."

Williams: "So I woke her up. I didn't hit her, I only hit her once Friday night." He looked up at the detective now directly into his eyes to make sure that the detective knew that the one time he had hit Jessica was the time he killed her.

Detective: "Okay."

Williams: "Well, so I raped her in her house. Then I took her to the car and I took her to Tweed. And then I spent the day in Tweed. And I hit her when we were walking, she thought we were leaving, I hit her in the back of the head."

Detective: "Okay."

Williams picked up his drink and held it for a minute. "Anything in particular?"

Detective: "What did the hit to the back of the head do?"

Williams still held the drink. He let out a short loud sigh and said, "Well, it surprised me. Her skull gave way. She was immediately unconscious, and then I strangled her."

Detective: "Okay. What did you hit her with?"

Williams: "Flashlight."

The detective picked up his drink and started to sip. "In the house or outside the house?"

Williams: "In the house. Yeah, they'll find signs of it."

Detective: "Where in the house did this happen?"

Williams then put his drink on the table and crossed his arms again. "In the main portion, right in front of the fireplace."

Detective: "What do you mean they'll find signs of it?"

Williams: "There was quite a bit of blood. I didn't expect it. I expected to knock her out. But obviously it generated a lot of blood."

Detective: "What did she bleed onto?"

Williams: "The floor, it's just tile floor."

Detective: "Did you clean it up?"

Williams: "I wiped it up, but I know it'll be easily spotted."

Detective: "What makes you think that? Like if I walked in that house now."

Williams: "Well, you're not going to see it, not at all. But the right substance will show it, I'm sure."

Detective: "Okay, um, so when that happened, did she have clothes on or was she naked?"

Williams: "She was dressed."

Detective: "So when we find her, is she going to have those clothes on, too?"

Williams: "Yep."

Detective: "Okay. Marie-France Comeau."

Williams: "There was an open window in the basement of her house when she was away. I went in there a couple of nights before she came home. I looked around. I went back in there around midnight when she was home. She was on the phone in her bedroom. She actually discovered me in the basement."

Williams again looked up into the detective's face with a tiny grin on his face. "She was trying to get her cat to come upstairs, and her cat was in the basement and had seen me, and it was fixated on me in the corner. She couldn't get the cat up, so she came downstairs to try and get the cat. I don't know why she came over towards me, I guess the cat was staring at me, and she was wondering what the cat was staring at." Williams put his head down facing his knees and went silent for a few minutes. "So when she spotted me, I had the same flashlight. I subdued her, tied her up, and brought her upstairs. And I strangled her later in the morning. Or more like suffocated her with some tape. Left her there."

Detective: "How did you subdue her, what do you mean by that, you subdued her in the basement?"

Williams: "Well, I had the same flashlight. She saw me right away, so I just hit her a couple of times around her head, try and knock her out. I didn't, but she was bleeding a little bit. Eventually through a struggle, I subdued her."

Detective: "All right. Any blood from that struggle?"

Williams: "Oh yeah, not a whole bunch, but that flashlight did break her skin a couple of times."

Detective: "Okay, what area of the basement did that take place in?"

Williams: "I was hiding behind the furnace, so she spotted me right there."

Detective: "Did she recognize you?"

Williams: "No, she didn't. I had a mask on my face."

Detective: "So you go upstairs, and you said she suffocated?"

Williams: "Well, she suffocated...I put tape on her mouth, then I put tape on her nose and held it there so she couldn't breathe."

Detective: "What kind of tape was it?"

Williams: "Duct tape."

Detective: "What happened to it?"

Williams: "Well, I took it with me and I can't remember what I did with that tape. I probably threw it in the garbage."

Detective: "Did you use tape for any other purposes?"

Williams: "No."

Detective: "Did she ever recognize you through this whole episode?" Williams adamantly shook his head no. "What did you say you had on your face?"

Williams: "I had just a cover for my head, you know, just a sports pullover type, like just a little cap kind of thing." Williams used his hands to try and show that he had some sort of toque that was large enough to pull over his face. "And just a head band over my nose and mouth. It covered most everything but my eyes."

Detective: "And this flashlight, where is it now?"

Williams: "In Tweed."

Detective: "In the house?"

Williams: "Yes."

Detective: "What kind of flashlight is it?"

Williams: "It's a red three double D, I'm not sure what brand it is, but it's metal or aluminum, it's like a big...I can't remember what brand it was. Anyway, it's a big one of those."

Detective: "Did you take anything out Marie-France's house or Jessica Lloyd's house?"

Williams: "Yep, some of their underwear."

Detective: "Okay, and where is that?"

Williams: "It's, um, in some boxes in the basement here in Ottawa. In the rec room. We just moved in, so there are boxes everywhere. Soon the same side as the furnished room, sort of the back wall."

Detective: "So what do the boxes look like?"

Williams: "I think one's a scanner, the box for my scanner. They're all right next to each other, so a quick look through the boxes, and they'll be there."

Detective: "How much underwear is in those boxes?"

Williams: "Sixty pieces or so."

Detective: "All women?"

Williams: "Yes, 60 pieces of theirs."

Detective: "Of whose?"

Williams: "Of Jessica's and Marie-France."

Detective: "So you took 60 pieces of the two women in total?"

Williams: "Yep."

Detective: "All right. When you talk about the scanner, it's in a scanner box?"

Williams: "My scanner is upstairs, its box is down in the basement, so it's inside that box."

Detective: "Okay. So does any of the underwear in that box belong to anyone else besides Marie-France Comeau and Jessica Lloyd?"

Williams: "Yep, there's some from each of the other two women."

Detective: "Okay. Why don't we talk about those other two women. So the first one happened on the 16th. I don't know why, but I can't recall their names. The lady that lived closer to you."

Williams: "Laurie was closer to me. So the first one, I had just spotted her and got into the house when she was asleep. Noticed that she was alone and just hit her with my hand while she was sleeping. Subdued her, mostly just by my weight. I had her take off her pajamas and took some pictures, took some of her underwear and left."

Detective: "And the other woman?"

Williams: "Same thing, yeah. I went through the back of the house. She was sleeping in her bedroom in front of the TV. Pretty much the same story."

Detective: "Anything different about that story? I mean pretty much the same story and exactly the same story are two different things."

Williams: "Yeah, no, not much different at all. I did have the flashlight that time, I hit her with the flashlight. But I didn't knock her out, I subdued her with my weight. I took off her clothes, took some pictures, and I left."

Detective: "Why do you think these things happen?"

Williams: "I don't know."

Detective: "Have you spent much time thinking about that?"

Williams: "About why?"

Detective: "Yeah."

Williams: "Yeah, but I don't have the answers. I'm pretty sure the answers don't matter."

Detective: "Let me ask you this. Did you like or dislike these women?"

Williams: "I didn't know any of them. I met Marie-France that one time in her airplane."

Detective: "When you go through these things...let's talk about Jessica because she was there with you for that whole day. What kinds of feeling were you experiencing when you were with her that day?"

Williams: "She was a very nice girl."

Detective: "Can you tell me why you killed her? Russ, do you know why you killed her?"

Williams: "Well, I think I killed her because I knew that her story would be recognized."

Detective: "Her story would be recognized? Tell me what you mean."

Williams: "Well, because she knew I was taking pictures. So because of the two stories in Tweed, I would have been fairly, you know, it would have been quite obvious."

Detective: "So if you didn't take pictures, what would you have done with her?"

Williams: "I don't know."

Detective: "Yeah, because she was at your house, right? Well, let me ask you this. Two lived, right? Two died. What was the difference in your mind between them?"

Williams: "Well, the attention the first two got was very much focused on the pictures I took. So anybody else telling stories about pictures would have been a fairly straight line."

Detective: "Okay, but when this thing happened with Marie-France, did you believe that you were already a suspect for what happened in Tweed?"

Williams: "No."

Detective: "So what were you concerned about?"

Williams: "Well, because I was pretty sure that she was serving military, right? It would have been difficult for investigators to ignore the connection."

Detective: "Okay, makes sense. Let's go back to Jessica then, okay? You see her on the Wednesday night on her treadmill; how do you see her?"

Williams: "She was in the basement, window wide open. I saw her then as I drove by."

Detective: "Did you stop to have a look at the house? How does that catch your eye as you drive by?"

Williams: "I was looking to see who was there. I don't know that area very well, so I was just keeping my eyes open."

Detective: "So you just spot her on the way. Did you keep going or did you stop and take a closer look that night or anything?"

Williams: "No."

Detective: "And you went back on the Thursday night, right?"

Williams: "Yep." He then stood up with his drink in his right hand and paced the floor a few times, before standing and resting his back against the wall near the corner of the room.

The detective continued to ask questions. "So you're back

on the Thursday night, and you went into the house before she came home?"

Williams remained standing in the corner and took a long drink before answering. "Yep, she was out."

Detective: "Nothing else?"

Williams: "Yep. She was out. I got in through the kitchen window, it was unlocked. Everything else was locked."

Detective: "So you were in there doing what?"

Williams: "Looking around, looking around to see who else lived in the house. It was just her."

Detective: "Then what do you do?"

Williams: "Well, I left the house and she came home. So I went to see if she was alone and she was. So I went in and she went to sleep."

Detective: "So you go in, and she's sleeping. Then what do you do?"

Williams: "Well, I snuck up to the side of her bed, expecting to try to knock her out, and she woke up. And she did as I said."

Detective: "What did you say?"

Williams: "I said, 'lie down on your tummy'."

Detective: "Okay."

Williams: "She did and I tied her up."

Detective: "What did you tie her up with?"

Williams: "Some rope that I had brought."

Detective: "So she's on her stomach; how are you tying her up?"

Williams: "Just tying her hands behind her back."

Detective: "Okay, she's got clothes on at that point?"

Williams nodded his head yes.

Detective: "What kind of clothes?"

Williams: "Sweats."

Detective: "All right. You tie her hands behind her back, and then what happens?"

Williams: "I took her clothes off." Williams walked back to the table and took a seat in his chair.

Detective: "Okay, and then what happened?"

Williams: "Then I raped her."

Detective: "Rape can mean a lot of different things. What kind of sexual act took place?"

Williams: "Just vaginal and oral."

Detective: "Oral, who was performing the oral sex?"

Williams: "Ummm, me on her and her on me."

Detective: "Any condoms used or anything like that?"

Williams: "No."

Detective: "Okay. Correct me if I'm wrong...vaginal intercourse, her performing oral sex on you, and you performing oral sex on her?"

Williams again shook his head yes.

Detective: "Do you remember what order those things occurred in?"

Williams: "Yep. I started with oral sex, then I raped her, then I made her perform oral sex on me."

Detective: "Okay, any kind of conversation happening when this was going on?"

Williams: "Yep, a little bit."

Detective: "What was being said?"

Williams: "I threatened her before she, before I had her perform oral sex."

Detective: "What did you say?"

Williams: "Well, I put a zip tie around her neck, and I said that I would pull it if..."

Detective: "Okay, so she did what you told her to do?"

Williams: "Yes."

Detective: "Any issues there? Any reason to pull it?" Williams shook his head no without saying anything. "Do you remember ejaculating at that point? Or at any point?"

Williams: "Not at that point, but later on."

Detective: "Okay. So the oral sex finishes, and then what happens next?"

Williams: "Well, I continued to rape her, and I had her put on some of her underwear. I took some pictures. Lots of pictures. Then I got her dressed and walked her back to the truck."

Detective: "At what point did you decide she was going to leave with you?"

Williams: "I'm not sure. That wasn't necessarily always the plan. But at some point, I was there for three hours, three and a bit."

Detective: "Okay, do you remember the conversation about leaving? Did she say anything about that?"

Williams: "No, she was certainly cooperative."

Detective: "Okay, cooperative can mean a number of different things. Was she excited about leaving with you?"

Williams looked up at the detective and laughed.

Detective: "I don't want to be sarcastic…"

Williams: "Oh, no, she just didn't put up much of a fuss."

Detective: "Did she try to negotiate with you at all, or?"

Williams: "No."

Detective: "What did she say?"

Williams: "Oh, I told her that I would let her go later on."

Detective: "So when you take her out of her house, was she still bound or how was that?"

Williams: "Just hands behind her back."

Detective: "What about her feet, anything there?"

Williams: "No, she was walking freely."

Detective: "Okay, barefoot?"

Williams: "No she had those brown suede shoes on that had been reported."

Detective: "So where does she sit in your truck, when she got to your truck?"

Williams: "Front seat, passenger side."

Detective: "And where do you go?"

Williams: "Straight to Tweed."

Detective: "Straight to your house in Tweed?"

Williams: "Yep."

Detective: "No stops?"

Williams: "Nope."

Detective: "What time was it, do you remember what time you arrived there?"

Williams: "I don't exactly, but I'd say between 4:30 and 5:30."

Detective: "Okay, when you were first there, before she came home, do you remember did anybody come to the door at all when you were at the house?"

Williams: "No. No, I think somebody had come to the house just before she did, I thought it was her, but they left. I was outside."

Detective: "Did you see who that person was? Or what kind of vehicle they were in or anything?"

Williams: "Nope. I saw the lights and thought it was her, then all of a sudden they left, I don't know what time."

Detective: "Okay. Where were you when that first vehicle pulled up?"

Williams: "In the back, backyard."

Detective: "So you didn't have a view of the vehicle, you could just tell there was a vehicle there, is that fair?"

Williams agreed by nodding his head but said nothing.

Detective: "So you get home 4:30 or 5 you say?"

Williams again moved his head up and down in agreement but said nothing.

Detective: "Then what happens?"

Williams: "Well, she had to go to the bathroom, and shower, wash her, then we went into my bedroom. Then we went to sleep a little bit, she was tied up."

Detective: "How was she tied up at that point?"

Williams: "Just her hands behind her back. I put tape over her eyes from the beginning, so that's what she had."

Detective: "When they find her, is that tape going to be there? Or was it ever removed?"

Williams: "No, I never removed it."

Detective: "What kind of tape?"

Williams: "Duct tape."

Detective: "The duct tape that you used, where is that roll?"

Williams: "It's all gone. I used the rest of it to bind her. It's on her body."

Detective: "So by all gone, is it with the body now?"

Williams again nodded in the affirmative, saying nothing.

Detective: "So you said you went to sleep when you got home? You had a shower, or you said she had a shower?"

Williams: "Well, we both got in, and I washed her off after she went to the bathroom. We both went to sleep, but she was tied up and I tied the rope to me, you know, so I could fall asleep a little bit and she couldn't move without waking me up."

Detective: "I'm trying to picture how that would be. So the rope's tied up to what on her?"

Williams: "It's tied to her hands behind her back, and then the rope just wrapped around me so there was no slack."

Detective: "Do you remember how long you slept for?"

Williams: "Uh, well, maybe a couple of hours."

Detective: "Do you know if she slept?"

Williams: "I don't know."

Detective: "So you wake up and?"

Williams: "It was...so we were up and down, so it wasn't

two hours straight. It was two hours in bed, there wasn't much sleep. Just lying there."

Detective: "So you get up from that and what happens next?"

Williams: "Umm, she had a seizure actually. She felt it coming on because she'd had some before. It lasted quite a while. I got her dressed and into the family room. Anyway, she, she recovered. She got...it was the stress. But it probably went on for about 15 minutes."

Detective: "So how do you know she had one before?"

Williams: "She told me."

Detective: "Did she tell you why she got them?"

Williams: "Well, she suggested it was stress. Yeah, so, she felt herself start to tense up, and she said she felt she was going to have a seizure. Yeah, so, she was having convulsions."

Detective: "So she recovered from that?"

Williams: "Yes, she...I stayed with her and talked her through it and made sure she didn't bite her tongue."

Detective: "Then what happened?"

Williams: "Well, we had a little lie down right there because she was exhausted. But I covered her and she went to sleep for an hour or so. And I had told her earlier that before I let her go, I wanted to take some pictures of her in her underwear and having sex with her. So after she had a rest for an hour or so, I had her put on a number of different of outfits she had."

Detective: "I'm sorry?"

Williams: "Put on a number of, you know, pairs of panties and bras that she had that I had taken from the house. So she put those on and I took pictures."

Detective: "Are you in any of these pictures?"

Williams: "Yep."

Detective: "What kind of images are you in?"

Strangely enough Williams looked up at the camera in the room that was filming the interrogation. This was the first time he had done that since he entered the room. Was it that he was thinking about who was watching him on the camera?

Williams: "Um, well, with her. On the hard drives, you'll see those as well. So there's video of, you know, almost four hours, I guess."

Detective: "Of what?"

Williams leaned over, picked up his cup and took another drink, trying to delay having to answer. "Well, of the...initially at her place, um, raping her." Williams started to get fidgety and move around a lot in his chair. "Yeah, so I was running the video and taking the pictures. So the video pretty much covers everything."

Detective: "Did you use video at other places?"

Williams: "Uh, at Marie-France's as well."

Detective: "Is that video on the hard drives? Same type of activity?"

Williams: "Yep. Only I didn't have her put on any of her stuff."

Detective: "So Jessica poses for these pictures and then what happens?"

Williams: "Then I got her dressed and she thought she was leaving, and then as we were walking out, I hit her on the back of the head."

Detective: "When did you decide to do that?"

There was another very long pause.

Williams: "The idea of striking her on the head was developed in the afternoon."

Detective: "And what was that strike supposed to accomplish? What was the intent of that strike?"

Williams: "Well, I thought that I'd be able to knock her out and I was going to strangle her."

Detective: "Okay. So when you actually do strike her, what's the result?"

Williams: "Her skull gave way a little bit and there was a lot of blood, so I think that's what happened, she was immediately unconscious. Then I strangled her."

Detective: "How did you strangle her?"

Williams: "The same rope. I just put it around her neck."

Detective: "Okay."

Williams: "While she was unconscious."

Detective: "What happened to the zip tie that was around her neck earlier?"

Williams: "I took it off around then, I guess."

Detective: "Did you take it off before you put the rope around her neck or after, or do you remember?"

Williams: "After she was dead."

Detective: "Okay, so the zip tie was around her neck while you used the rope?" Williams nodded yes again. "Did you leave the rope around her neck?"

Williams: "No."

Detective: "And how did you know that she was dead?"

Williams: "She, um, well, her body stopped moving."

Detective: "So what did you do after that?"

Williams: "I bound her up in a fetal position, and cleaned up the floor."

Detective: "When you bound her all up, was that with the duct tape you were referring to earlier?"

Williams: "Yep."

Detective: "So then what did you do?"

Williams: "I put her in the garage. It was very cold. Then I went in to the base."

Detective: "Why did you go to the base?"

Williams: "Because I was flying early the next morning."

Detective: "Okay. So what time did you leave to go to the base?"

Williams: "I told you, between 9 and 10 or so."

Detective: "On the Friday night?"

Williams: "Yep."

Detective: "So you fly and — "

Williams: "Then I drove home to Ottawa."

Detective: "So which night would you —"

Williams: "Saturday night."

Detective: "So you land, what time are you landing?"

Williams: "Six or 6:30 Saturday night."

Detective: "Did you go by the house in Tweed on your way to Ottawa?"

Williams shook his head no.

Detective: "So you drove straight home to Ottawa?"

Williams continued to say nothing and now shook his head yes.

Detective: "What time did you get there at, do you remember?"

Williams: "Sometime before midnight. I can't remember, but I think I went in to the office first and did some work, so I didn't get home before midnight. I think, I'm not sure, I slept for a little bit in the Tim Horton's in Brockville. So it may be later, I can't honestly remember when I got home. Midnight-ish."

Detective: "So you get home in Ottawa, what do you do, go to bed?"

Williams: "Yeah."

Detective: "So what do you do the next day?"

Williams: "My wife and I did some stuff, I can't remember what was going on that day. Putting together the new house. I headed back to Tweed that night. Sorry...um." Then Williams looked up to the sky and seemed to be thinking for a while. "No, I didn't, I had Monday off, that's right. I had Monday off, and I was visiting one of the units in Ottawa on Tuesday. So I headed back to Tweed on Tuesday night."

Detective: "You headed back to Tweed and what happens next?"

Williams: "I took Jessica's body to that spot."

Detective: "That happened on Tuesday night. Just this past Tuesday obviously."

Williams continued to shake his head yes.

Detective: "Do you remember what time that was?"

Williams: "It was pretty late, it was midnight-ish. I'd say between midnight and one on Wednesday morning."

Detective: "What made you decide to measure that distance, the 0.7 kilometers?"

Williams: "That's just the way I am with numbers, I have to know the numbers."

Detective: "And how did you leave her?"

Williams: "I just left her behind a very large rock."

Detective: "Is that duct tape still on her?"

Williams again nodded his head yes, saying nothing.

Detective: "What else is on her?"

Williams: "A couple of towels wrapped around her head, and the top and pants that she was wearing. Jeans."

Detective: "Did you ever go back there?"

Williams: "Nope."

Detective: "What other type of cleaning and things like that did you do? Anything else to kind of cover your tracks that you can think of?"

Williams: "I vacuumed the house and I wiped the floor, washed the floor."

Detective: "What about your truck, did you do anything with that?"

Williams: "Just washed it, it was a mess, and vacuumed."

Detective: "So Marie-France. When did it first occur to you to go to her house?"

Williams: "Probably in October. October or November. I can't quite remember, but probably in that time frame."

Detective: "Do you remember why, why you thought to do that?"

Williams: "Well, she lived alone. The one time I met her..."

Detective: "I wish I had a why her versus the dozens of other women you probably come across on a daily basis."

Williams: "I don't know. I went out there when she wasn't home, just to see where she lived."

Detective: "When did you do that?"

Williams: "A couple of nights before."

Detective: "How did you know her address?"

Williams: "From the base."

Detective: "So when you go out there a couple of nights before, do you remember what night that was? When you were there the first time?"

Williams: "I don't, but it was within two or three nights. No more than four."

Detective: "Did you actually go into her house on that occasion, or —?"

Williams: "Yes."

Detective: "What happened that night? How did you get into her house?"

Williams: "This window in the side of the basement, side window."

Detective: "Just to back step a bit, how did you get to her

house that night?"

Williams: "I drove."

Detective: "What did you drive?"

Williams: "I drove my truck."

Detective: "Pathfinder?"

Williams: "Yes."

Detective: "Do you remember where you parked it?"

Williams: "Yep. I parked it in a little bit of a division in the residential area there. I parked it on the other side, 6 or 700 hundred meters away."

Detective: "So not on her street? Do you remember what street you were on?"

Williams: "No. It might be the same street, but there's an interruption in the street, where there's construction zones. There's a pathway in between, so I think it's probably the same street."

Detective: "So you go to her house, and when you went there that night, did you know that she was away?"

Williams: "I'm not sure if I knew entirely, but I think I thought she was away."

Detective: "Is that based on her schedule, or how would you know?"

Williams: "Yeah. Because I fly with the squadron, I have access to the schedule. It's a slightly different schedule she had, that's probably how I knew."

Detective: "You don't know for sure?"

Williams: "I think that's probably where I got it."

Detective: "So you go over to her house, and what do you do the first night?"

Williams: "Well, I looked around to make sure that she was living alone."

Detective: "I am sorry, did you say how you got in?"

Williams: "The same way, the side basement window."

Detective: "Do you remember what kind of window it was?"

Williams: "I just noticed that it was not locked, it was open slightly. So I just moved the screen, slid it open, and went in."

Detective: "So you go in and you're in her house, find out that she was living alone. So did you do anything that night?"

Williams: "Yeah, I was playing with her underwear."

Detective: "What do you mean playing with her underwear?"

Williams: "Well, wearing it."

Detective: "Doing anything else?"

Williams: "No, I didn't touch her stuff."

Detective: "What do you mean didn't touch her stuff? I mean, you touched her underwear."

Williams: "Yeah, but nothing else."

Detective: "Did you take any of her underwear with you that night?"

Williams: "Yep, a few pieces."

Detective: "Where did you find the underwear when you went in?"

Williams: "Her drawer."

Detective: "Was it clean or was it used?"

Williams: "Clean."

Detective: "Anything else that you remember doing that evening?"

Williams: "No."

Detective: "So after that first visit, did you return again before being there with her?"

Williams: "No."

Detective: "So which day did you go to her house, when she was there?"

Williams: "Well, the night before I went to Ottawa, so I think it was Monday night."

Detective: "So let's walk through that night. What time did you get there?"

Williams: "About 11 or so, probably 10 to 11." Williams took another long pause. "She was on the phone in her room. I could hear that from the back yard. I got in through the side window."

Detective: "The same basement window?"

Williams: "Yes."

Detective: "What could you hear her from the backyard?"

Williams: "I heard her on the phone." Williams stood up again and started to walk back and forth, stretching his back. "I was beside the house, and I could hear her through the walls on the phone."

Detective: "Any idea who she was talking to, or what she was talking about?"

Williams: "Nope, I couldn't hear that well."

Detective: "Okay. So you go in through the basement window, and what are you wearing when this was happening?"

Williams: "Um, a sweat shirt and Dockers, I guess. And the two pieces on my head."

Detective: "So where are those two pieces now? The pieces that you wore on the head."

Williams: "They're probably in my bag in, my luggage bag, and it's in the bedroom."

Detective: "What's your luggage bag look like?"

Williams: "It's a blue duffel bag type thing. It's right beside the bed."

Detective: "It's the only blue duffel bag in your bedroom?"

Williams: "Yes."

Detective: "These pieces, what do they look like again?"

Williams: "It's a blue headband. It's a standard blue winter headband. And a black skull cap type thing."

Detective: "Any insignia or anything on them?"

Williams: "Yeah, there are, but I don't know what they are. The blue headband has something, a name of some sort stitched on it. And the skull cap has some sort of emblem, white emblem on the black. I don't know what it is."

Detective: "Are they sport emblems, or company emblems?"

Williams: "It's the manufacturers."

Detective: "Anything else in the blue duffel bag?"

Williams: "I think so."

Detective: "Is it full of things other?"

Williams: "Just my clothes."

Detective: "You go in, do you remember what you had on your feet?"

Williams: "In the house there?"

Detective: "When you went to MarieFrance's house."

Williams: "Probably rain shoes, there wasn't snow on the ground."

Detective: "So you go in, you're in the basement, and whereabouts in the basement are you?"

Williams: "By the furnace."

Detective: "And what are you doing? What's your plans at that point?"

Williams: "I was waiting for her to go to bed."

Detective: "And how long did that take?"

Williams: "Well, she didn't, because she came down looking for the cat."

Detective: "Right, so what happens next?"

Williams: "As I described earlier, I subdued her. Hit her with the flashlight." Williams walked back over to the table, picked up his cup and took another drink. He put down the cup and walked back to where he was standing and continued to explain. "Essentially, I threw her to the ground and tied her up."

Detective: "What did you use to tie her up?"

Williams: "The same rope, the green rope. It's in Tweed."

Detective: "Is it just green? How long is the piece of rope?"

Williams: "It's probably 20 feet. It's a boat rope. It's got some red specks in it I think." Williams walked back and sat in his chair again. He seemed quite a bit calmer now, not so uncomfortable.

Detective: "Is there lots of ropes in Tweed, or is this probably the only rope?"

Williams: "No, this, there are two lengths."

Detective: "Two lengths of the same green rope?"

Williams: "Yes."

Detective: "And were they both used?"

Williams: "Uh, well, I only ever had one with me, so I don't know if I used the same piece both times or not, but there's only two and one is the rope."

Detective: "So you tie her up, how did you tie her up?"

Williams: "In the back."

Detective: "And what is she wearing at that point?"

Williams: "She wasn't wearing anything to start with."

Detective: "So when she came down into the basement, she had no clothes on?"

Williams: "Yes, she had some sort of a shawl around her shoulder. She immediately dropped it when she saw me."

Detective: "Did she say anything when she saw you?"

Williams: "She did. She called out, 'You bastard!'"

Detective: "Okay, and then what happened?"

Williams: "And then I subdued her as I described."

Detective: "By hitting her with that red flashlight?"

Williams: "Yes. All were glancing blows, they cut her skin, but didn't do much else. She fell over, then I subdued her. She tripped."

Detective: "How did you tie her up at that point? Like, I know you used the rope, but what did you tie her up like?"

Williams: "I just pulled her hands behind her back and I tied her wrists together."

Detective: "Then what happened after that?"

Williams: "Then I took her upstairs."

Detective: "Did she go upstairs on her own power, or did you carry her?"

Williams: "No, she passed out on the stairs, and I carried her up."

Detective: "Why do you think she passed out?"

Williams: "I expect from the hits to her head."

Detective: "So you carried her up to where?"

Williams: "To her bedroom and I put her on her bed."

Detective: "Then what happened?"

Williams: "Well, as I described, I think, she's on the bed. I raped her over a period of time."

Detective: "And again, to be specific what sex acts took place?"

Williams: "Just vaginal."

Detective: "Your penis in her vagina?"

Williams: "Yep."

Detective: "Any condom use?"

Williams: "Nope."

Detective: "Did you ejaculate?"

Williams: "No."

Detective: "Did you ejaculate at any point with her?"

Williams: "Nope."

Detective: "Just before I forget, I think I asked you, I don't mean to bounce around here, Russ, but Jessica. I asked you about ejaculation and you said you didn't at that point. So when did you ejaculate with Jessica?"

Williams: "Um, the second time or the third time that I had her perform oral sex."

Detective: "And was that at your residence or hers?"

Williams: "Hers."

Detective: "Any other times you ejaculated with her?"

Williams: "No."

Detective: "When you ejaculated with Jessica, did you use anything to clean up?"

Williams: "No."

Detective: "What happened to the ejaculate?"

Williams: "She swallowed it."

Detective: "So getting back to Marie-France, so it was just straight vaginal sex? No condoms, no ejaculation, right?"

Williams: "Yes."

Detective: "How long does that go for? How long were you engaged in that activity?"

Williams: "Uh, a couple, well, hour and a half or two hours, I guess."

Detective: "And then what happens next?"

Williams: "Well as I described, I suffocated her with tape."

Detective: "Why did you decide to do that?"

Williams then bent over. Now he seemed to be getting upset with the questions. "Well, again, because of the pictures as I described to you, and it was going to be a pretty straight line back to Tweed."

Detective: "But why did you decide to use that method versus something else?"

Williams: "I thought about strangling her earlier. It's on video."

Detective: "What is?"

Williams: "It was a short-lived attempt as she struggled quite a bit. Then I decided that I needed to suffocate her.

Detective: "So a short-lived attempt at strangling her?"

Williams: "Yes."

Detective: "And what's on the video? The suffocation or the strangling?"

Williams: "Just me putting my hand on her throat. And then her responding. A surprise. Very aggressively."

Detective: "Now, you mentioned you brought the rope with you; where did the duct tape come from?"

Williams: "I brought it."

Detective: "Okay, and what did you do with it afterwards?"

Williams: "I think it stayed in Tweed."

Detective: "What color of duct tape are we talking about? I know it comes in a variety of colors."

Williams: "Grey."

Detective: "Grey. Okay, so before the suffocation, obviously, how long do you think you were with her from the point. How long to do think you were in that house from the point you went in that window until you left?"

Williams got up slowly and picked up his cup again, and started to pace back and forth. "Probably four hours."

Detective: "So correct me if I'm wrong, you say you got there at 11, or around 11?"

Williams: "I think that's right."

Detective: "So you left around three?"

Williams: "Well, I was in the basement for quite a while before she came down, and she wasn't going to bed. So I was probably in the basement for 30 or 40 minutes."

Detective: "Okay."

Williams: "So by the time she saw me, it was probably closer to midnight. But I didn't have a watch on, so I'm not sure."

Detective: "Any gloves?"

Williams put his cup down on the table, but continued to

pace back and forth. "I don't think so."

Detective: "Did you wear gloves with Jessica?"

Williams: "Only to get in the house. It was a very cold night."

Detective: "What about the two women in Tweed?"

Williams: "No gloves."

Detective: "So while you're with Marie-France, what kind of conversations are taking place? Anything she said to you stick out in your mind?"

Williams: "No, I had taped her mouth; there was no conversation."

Detective: "Okay, when did you tape her mouth?"

Williams: "As soon as I got her up to the bedroom."

Detective: "Why did you decide to do that?"

Williams: "Because she was, you know, quite aggressive."

Detective: "In what way?"

Williams: "I'm confident she would have screamed if given a chance, because she did initially."

Detective: "Did she?"

Williams: "In the basement."

Detective: "So in what way was she aggressive?"

Williams: "Well, just when she discovered me, she was very vocal, screamed quite a bit until I subdued her, so I expected she'd scream again if given the chance."

Detective: "Do you remember how you left her residence?"

Williams: "The back door, a patio door."

Detective: "Did you take anything with you that night?"

Williams: "Some of her underwear."

Detective: "Anything else?" Williams shook his head no. "Well, okay, did you do anything else to try and cover your tracks with Marie-France?"

Williams: "Well, I turned off my Blackberry before I left Trenton. Other than that, no."

Detective: "Do you remember trying to destroy any evidence there, or anything that you thought may have produced evidence or anything?"

Williams: "I took her sheets off the bed and ran them through the laundry."

Detective: "The laundry where?"

Williams: "In her house."

Detective: "Did you run them completely through? Did you wait for them to finish?"

Williams: "No, I just put them in, and put a whole bunch of bleach in and let it go."

Detective: "So the night you went to her place and got there at 11, you came from where? Like, you said you left Trenton, turned off your Blackberry. Were you talking about the base or where did you leave to go to her house?"

Williams: "Well, no. I just turned off my Blackberry before I left the Trenton area. I would have left from the base after work."

Detective: "All right. What time do you think you turned your Blackberry off?"

Williams: "Well, it's only a half hour drive, so probably in the 9 or 9:30 range."

Detective: "Do you remember what time you turned it back on?"

Williams: "No. I was back on the 401 heading back to Ottawa the next morning."

Detective: "What time would have that been?"

Williams: "Six, plus or minus 30 minutes."

Detective: "So you leave her house three-ish,"

Williams: "No I think it was later than that. The four hours was obviously, I think I entered at 11, was in the basement quite a while, so I think I left her house at 4 or 4:30 somewhere around there."

Detective: "Okay, and where do you go?"

Williams: "I drove to Ottawa."

Detective: "Straight to Ottawa?"

Williams: "Yep."

Detective: "Did you stop by your house in Tweed or anything, or did you go straight home?"

Williams: "Yes."

Detective: "Do you remember what route you took?"

Williams: "Yep. The 401, but from her place, I think I went straight north on whatever the road is that goes through Brighton, up to the 401. Took the 401 and headed east."

Detective: "And so you're going to, what's the meeting you're having that day in Ottawa, remind me?"

Williams: "The meeting on the acquisition of the C-17."

Detective: "Who went to that meeting?"

Williams: "The project manager, Miss Sue Hale."

Detective: "Is that the only meeting around that time period that would have happened on that issue with Sue Hale?"

Williams: "Yes."

Detective: "There wasn't a weekly meeting or stuff like that?"

Williams: "No, it was sort of quarterly."

Detective: "Okay. So the night you went, the night this happened, where did you park that night?"

Williams: "Like I said, on the gravel, it's probably the same road."

Detective: "Similar location to the first night?"

Williams: "Yep."

Detective: "Same vehicle?"

Williams: "Yep, my truck."

Detective: "Let's talk about, seeing as we're going backward in time, let's talk about the second incident in Tweed with Laurie Massicotte. The one that's at 76 Cosy Cove. How did you decide on her?"

Williams: "I knew she lived alone, that's it."

Detective: "How did you know that?"

Williams: "She lived three doors down, and I didn't know her but I knew she had a boyfriend, and he hadn't been around, so I looked in the window and she was alone."

Detective: "So she had a boyfriend that wasn't too frequent?"

Williams: "Well, she told me that they were fighting. That's why he hadn't been around."

Detective: "So did you look in her house the night that this was about to happen?"

Williams: "I had been in within the week, probably a couple of nights earlier."

Detective: "What did you do that night?"

Williams: "I looked around to see if there were any current signs of her boyfriend, I guess. I took one or two pieces of her underwear. That's all."

Detective: "Okay, so the night you go there and the incident happens, do you remember what time that was?"

Williams: "That was pretty late. I probably got into the

house around midnight. She was asleep on the couch, I didn't know that, but I knew she was in there."

Detective: "How did you get in?"

Williams: "A window in the back of the house. It was a little sun room."

Detective: "Was it something you just had to slide or how did you get in?"

Williams: "I removed the screen and slid the window. So I got into the house and she was sleeping on the couch in front of the TV."

Detective: "Were you wearing anything on your face that night?"

Williams: "Yep, same things."

Detective: "The headband and the cap?"

Williams looked at the detective and shook his head yes.

Detective: "What kind of clothes did you have on?"

Williams: "Just a dark sweatshirt and pants."

Detective: "So she was asleep on the couch, you're in there, what happens?"

Williams: "We have been through, eh?"

Detective: "I know."

Williams: "I struck her with the flashlight thinking it would knock her out. It didn't. We struggled. I subdued her, took some pictures, and left. I was in the house about two-and-a-half hours."

Detective: "That's a pretty short description for two-and-a-half hours."

Williams: "Well, we talked. I told her I wasn't going to hurt her. I told her that there were other guys in the house robbing her. My job was just to control her."

Detective: "What did she say to that?"

Williams: "She was scared. Worried she was going to get seriously hurt."

Detective: "Did she say that or did you assume that?"

Williams: "No, she said that she was worried she was going to be killed. I told her I'm not going to kill anyone."

Detective: "You said you took pictures of her. Clothed or unclothed?"

Williams: "Both. Clothed and unclothed."

Detective: "Are you in any of those pictures?"

Williams: "I don't think so."

Detective: "You just took them of her?"

Williams: "Yes."

Detective: "What kind of camera are you using, by the way?"

Williams: "It's a digital Sony."

Detective: "You just have the one camera?"

Williams: "Yep. And the video camera."

Detective: "Oh, so they're two separates?"

Williams: "Yep."

Detective: "Well, some cameras take video, right? And where is that camera and the video camera?"

Williams: "In Tweed."

Detective: "They are the only camera and video camera in that house?"

Williams: "Yep."

Detective: "All right. So you take pictures of her, and how do you end up leaving?"

Williams: "I just told her to count and wait for a number of minutes, I don't know, before she called the police."

Detective: "Did you leave immediately or did you stay there for a while?"

Williams: "No, I left."

Detective: "And where do you go?"

Williams: "Home."

Detective: "Straight home?"

Williams: "Yeah."

Detective: "Did you wait and see if the police showed up?"

Williams: "Nope. I mean, it's only a couple hundred feet."

Detective: "So what did you do when you got home?"

Williams: "I went to sleep."

Detective: "So what did you do the next day?"

Williams: "Went in to work a couple of hours later."

Detective: "Do you remember how her clothing was removed?"

Williams: "Well, because her hands were tied behind her back, I would have cut off her top and pulled off her bottom."

Detective: "What did you use to cut off her top?"

Williams: "I can't remember if it was a knife or folding X-Acto knife or Leatherman or one of the two."

Detective: "Are these items in your house in Tweed?"

Williams: "Yep."

Detective: "Was there any other time that you used a knife to cut off clothing or anything else, do you remember?"

Williams: "I cut off Jessica's top with a knife because her hands were tied behind her back. That's all."

Detective: "Where is that knife? Which knife did you use?"

Williams: "That was the Leatherman. It's in Tweed."

Detective: "Is it the only Leatherman in Tweed?"

Williams: "Yes."

Detective: "So on September 16, when you went in that night, was it the first time you'd been in her house?"

Williams: "Yep."

Detective: "Okay, and why her?"

Williams: "Just because I had seen her and she was cute. That's it."

Detective: "So there was no...you didn't go into her house before that?"

Williams: "Nope."

Detective: "So you go in, and how did you get into her house?"

Williams: "The side window was not locked, so I cut the screen, slid open the window, and crawled in."

Detective: "What were you wearing?"

Williams: "Same sweatshirt and dark pants."

Detective: "The same hat and —?"

Williams: "Yes."

Detective: "And where did you find her?"

Williams: "In bed sleeping."

Detective: "And what do you do?"

Williams: "I stood over her for a while and I hit her on the left side of her head with my hand. I just woke her up, she struggled. You know, I'd just lay on her, pretty much how I described a little bit ago. Took off her, I pulled her top down, and took off her pants, took some pictures and left."

Detective: "Do you remember her saying anything to you?"

Williams: "Yes."

Detective: "What did she say to you?"

Williams: "Tons of things, you know. She had a young baby just next door, the other room, eight months or so. I was obviously concerned about the baby. She was concerned for herself, so I assured her I was not going to hurt her. That's basically all."

Detective: "Any underwear taken from Laurie?"

Williams: "Sure."

Detective: "And where would they be located?"

Williams: "In Tweed."

Detective: "Why are they in Tweed, as opposed to Marie-France and Jessica's underwear?"

Williams: "I don't know."

Detective: "Do you remember how much of their underwear you took?"

Williams: "Not very much from Laurie."

Detective: "Did they know that you took their underwear?"

Williams: "I don't know."

Detective: "You didn't discuss it with them or anything?"

Williams: "No."

Detective: "So where in Tweed would their underwear be?"

Williams: "In the, there's a laundry room area."

Detective: "Okay."

Williams: "Just between the house and the garage."

Detective: "So where in the laundry room area would they be kept?"

Williams: "There's a cupboard up top. They are in a duffel bag."

Detective: "What does the duffel bag look like?"

Williams: "It's a green army duffel bag."

Detective: "Okay. Are they all in the same duffel bag?"

Williams: "Yes."

Detective: "Is there anything else in that duffel bag?"

Williams: "Just underwear."

Detective: "Okay."

Williams reached over to the table where his cup was and took another drink. He then got up and started to pace again.

Detective: "When these pictures are looked at, you talked about being in Marie-France's underwear on the first night you went in. Did you take photographs of that?"

Williams: "Yep."

Detective: "What about anybody else's underwear?"

Williams: "Yep."

Detective: "Where were those photos taken?"

Williams: "Well, sometimes in...In Marie-France's case, in her house. The others, in my house."

Detective: "In Tweed."

Williams: "Yes."

Detective: "So you would take the underwear back and then at some point put the underwear on and take pictures?"

Williams: "Yeah."

Detective: "What about Jessica's underwear?"

Williams: "Uh, she's...only her and Marie-France."

Detective: "So you have pictures of you and her?"

Williams: "Yep."

Detective: "Well, I guess I only have a couple of questions for you. I'm sure there's going to be more questions for you. I guess what's on my mind right now is what made you decide to tell me about this tonight?"

Williams: "Mostly to make my wife's life easier."

Detective: "Is what you told me tonight the truth?"

Williams: "Yes."

Detective: "How do you feel about what you've done?"

Williams: "Disappointed."

Detective: "Let me ask you this. If this didn't come to the point that it is right now, if for whatever reason you didn't show up on our radar, so to speak, do you think it would have happened again?"

Williams: "I was hoping not, but I can't answer the question."

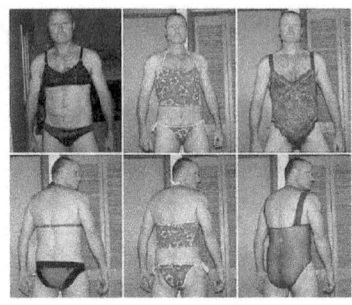

Williams admits to wearing his victims underwear and taking pictures of himself

BREAK FOR ONE HOUR

When the detective came back in the room, it was about one hour later. Russell was still standing where he was when the detective left the room. The detective put his binder of papers on the table and opened it up.

Detective: "Not too much here, Russ, just a few details that I wanted to cover off. Specifically, with Marie-France. In the basement of her house, there's a hole in the dry wall, do you recall how that happened?"

Williams now took a seat and faced the detective directly with a very serious look on his face.

Williams: "Where about?"

Detective: "I don't know specifically, but it's downstairs."

Williams: "I don't remember that, no."

Detective: "Okay, do you remember doing anything with her in the basement where you may have used some clothing or something like that to secure her?"

Williams: "Yep, I tied her up against one of the poles in the basement initially. I went back outside and put the screen back on and secured the window."

Detective: "While she was tied to the pole?"

Williams: "Yep."

Detective: "And what was your thinking behind doing that, at that point?"

Williams: "Just to show where her assailant had come in."

Detective: "Now, by the time that she was tied to that pole, was that in the very initial first few minutes of the confrontation?"

Williams: "That was shortly after I subdued her and tied her up, yes."

Detective: "Does she have the duct tape on her mouth yet?"

Williams: "I think probably. The pictures will show it."

Detective: "Okay, now in the upstairs bathroom, by her bedroom, there's a, it looks like something occurred in there. Do you remember that?"

Williams: "Yep."

Detective: "What happened there?"

Williams: "She had passed out in bed, and I went to look

and see if anybody was coming, and she got up and closed the bedroom door, and raced into the bathroom trying to get somebody's attention. But her mouth was taped and her hands were tied."

Detective: "What did you do as a result of that?"

Williams: "Well, I just got back in the room and subdued her again, and got her back in, regained control of her again."

Detective: "There was blood in there. Do you know how that would have occurred?"

Williams: "It's from the initial hits, as I was trying to subdue her. The blows to her head."

Detective: "Okay. Do you recall blood being in the bathroom?"

Williams: "No. I actually didn't have a light on in there. But it doesn't surprise me." Detective: "There's a pair of underwear and some socks on the floor of the bathroom that belong to her. Do you remember how they got in there?"

Williams: "No. I didn't see them."

Detective: "What do you recall doing to her breasts? It's pretty clear that there was something that happened to her breasts. Do you recall?"

Williams looked up at the detective with a real curious look on his face, like he didn't have a clue what the detective was talking about, and shook his head no. "I certainly touched her breasts, but I didn't do anything to hurt them."

Detective: "You don't remember that?"

Williams: "No. When I suffocated her she was on her front, so there may have been something there."

Detective: "What do you mean?"

Williams: "Well, she was lying on the floor when I suffocated her, and we obviously struggled. It may have been in there that something happened. But I didn't do something specific to her breasts."

Detective: "When you suffocated her, that's when you had the duct tape over her mouth and nose?"

Williams: "Yes."

Detective: "That was on the floor?"

Williams: "Yes."

Detective: "So what happened after that?"

Williams: "Well, she died, and then I took the tape off her head and put her on the bed. I covered her up with the duvet."

Detective: "What was your thinking behind doing that?"

Williams: "I don't know."

Detective: "As you might have expected, Russ, certainly even now, one of the Ottawa investigators mentioned to me, there's a number of incidents that have gone unsolved over the years."

Williams: "Can I go to the washroom quickly?"

10

IS THAT WHAT I THINK IT IS?

Sergeant Smyth provided Williams with a pad of paper and a pen, with a suggestion that he write some letters of apology to his victims. This was not merely an apology for the families of the victims, this was also a police tactic to help prevent a claim of false confession by the charged. Smyth left the room and gave Williams about a half an hour. When he returned, Williams had written nothing. So Smyth pressed him again and told him that this was his last chance, and then left the room again. When the officer returned, Williams had written a total of eight letters.

LETTER ONE

To Mary Harriman (Williams' wife):

"I love you, sweet (unreadable). I am so very sorry for having hurt you like this. I know you'll take good care of sweet Rosie (their cat). I love you, Russ."

LETTER TWO

To Roxanne Lloyd (mother of murder victim Jessica Lloyd):

"Mrs. Lloyd, you won't believe me, I know, but I am sorry for having taken your daughter from you. Jessica was a beautiful, gentle young woman, as you know. I know she loved you very much, she told me so, again and again. I can tell you that she did not suspect that the end was coming. Jessica was happy because she believed that she was coming home. I know you have already had a lot of pain in your life. I am sorry to have caused you so much more."

LETTER THREE

Another draft to Mrs. Lloyd:

"I know you won't believe me, but I am sorry for having taken your daughter from you. Jessica was a beautiful, gentle young woman. I know she loved you very much. Though I forced her to have sex..."

IS THAT WHAT I THINK IT IS? | 177

He then scribbled through the lines and stopped writing that letter.

LETTER FOUR

Another draft to Mrs. Lloyd:

"Mrs. Lloyd, you won't believe me, I know, but I am sorry for having taken your daughter from you. Jessica was a beautiful, gentle young woman. I know she loved you very much, because she told me again and again. The moment she died she was quite happy, because she believed that I was going to let her go. She did not know what was coming."

Again, he scribbled through this letter and stopped writing.

LETTER FIVE

To the undisclosed sexual assault victim

"I apologize for having traumatized you the way did. No doubt you'll sleep a bit easier now that I've been caught."

LETTER SIX

To Laurie Massicotte (second sexual assault victim)

"Laurie, I am sorry for having hurt you the way I did. I really hope that the discussion we had has helped you turn your life around a bit. You seem like a bright woman who could do much better for herself. I do hope you find a way to succeed."

LETTER SEVEN

To Ernie Comeau, father of murder victim Marie-France Comeau

"Mr. Comeau, I am sorry for having taken your daughter, Marie-France, from you. I know you won't be able to believe me, but it is true. Marie-France has been deeply missed by all who knew her."

LETTER EIGHT

To Mr. Comeau, a different draft.

"Mr. Comeau, I am sorry for having taken your daughter from you. I know you won't be able to believe me, but it is the case. I know she has been deeply missed by all who knew her."

Again, he scribbled through the lines he had written and stopped writing.

Early the next morning, Williams led investigators to Jessica Lloyd's body in a secluded area on Cary Road, 13 minutes away from where he lived. Williams was also charged in the death of Corporal Marie-France Comeau, the 37-year-old military flight attendant based at CFB Trenton who had been found dead inside her home in late November 2009.

Along with the murder charges, Williams was charged with breaking and entering, forcible confinement, and the sexual assault of two other women in two separate home invasions near Tweed, Ontario in September 2009. Per reports, the women had been bound in their homes and the attacker had taken photos of them.

Williams was arraigned and remanded into custody on Monday, February 8, 2010. The Canadian Forces announced that day that an interim commander would soon be appointed to replace him (Dave Cochrane took over 11 days later), and removed his biography from the Department of National Defense website the following day.

Hours after the announcement of Williams's arrest, police services across the country reopened unsolved homicide cases involving young women in areas where Williams, a career military man, had previously been stationed. Per news reports, police began looking at other unsolved cases based on a full statement that Williams gave to police.

Sergeant Smyth was soon granted a warrant, permitting officers to search Williams's cottage on February 11, 2010. Mary Elizabeth, Williams's wife, had been at home when the police arrived to search with warrant in hand. Harriman was given time to gather her things and leave before they began their search. Detective Sergeant Brian Mason oversaw executing the search warrant. It seemed like an army of police swarmed the residence. In total, there were 12 officers and forensic specialists who arrived in two vans.

During the seven days it took for the police to conduct their search of the cottage, police found red stains consistent with blood on a drawer of the dresser in the master bedroom, on a chair in the living room, and in the bathtub.

The tapes and memory card that contained video footage and pictures of the assaults and rapes on both Marie-France Comeau and Jessica Lloyd were found in a vestibule at the bottom of the piano. Police also found electrical and duct tape, rope, black zip ties, and a duffel bag that was stored in the laundry room cupboard. Inside the duffel bag, there were eight more smaller plastic bags. Here is a listing of what was in each of those bags:

BAG #1

- 93 pairs of women's panties
- 1 slip

BAG #2

- 4 camisoles
- 6 tops
- 13 dresses
- 1 T-shirt

BAG #3

- 2 women's bathing suits
- 2 bikini bottoms
- 8 pairs of panties
- 1 pair of tights
- 18 camisoles
- 1 pair of fishnet stockings
- 1 garter
- 1 garter belt

BAG #4

- 1 nightie
- 1 panty-and-camisole set
- 1 camisole

- 1 pair of panties
- 1 slip

BAG #5

- 51 pairs of panties

BAG #6

- 35 pairs of panties

BAG #7

- 77 pairs of panties
- 3 bathing suit tops
- 2 bras
- 1 bikini bottom
- 2 socks

BAG #8

- 49 bras

IS THAT WHAT I THINK IT IS? | 183

Found in William's home during police search

In addition to the eight smaller bags of women's garments, the police also found an assortment of sex toys and a 4" x 6" picture of his first assault victim.

It brought up an interesting thought: How, when these items were stored in such a way where Williams's wife could so easily have come across them, was she not aware of what he was doing? How would he have possibly explained them to her? Not to mention all the bloodstains found throughout the house. Another point is why wasn't he trying to hide the items from her? Was he just not worried about what she thought?

The police also found and seized several items from the home:

- Book titled *LSI Guide to Lock Picking*
- Sony digital camera
- Colonel Air Force flight suits
- A KRK systems box which contained female underwear and a Ziploc bag full of lubricants
- An APC battery backup box which contained four vibrators, a DVD titled *Real Sex Home Videos*, six

batteries, 14 pairs of panties, 34 bras, 2 camisoles, and 1 slip
- Computers and associated equipment, which included two external hard drives that had explicit videos and photos of Williams's attacks on both Comeau and Lloyd, as well as a detailed spread sheet of Williams's crimes
- A black skull cap
- Pillowcase with 5 pairs of panties, 1 bra, 2 vibrators, pajama bottoms, a slip, and 2 pairs of children's panties
- A green camera bag containing a Sony camera and a pair of women's underwear
- An Epson computer printer box that had 15 pairs of women's panties, 5 bras, a tube of KY jelly, 8 photographs of Jessica Lloyd, Jessica Lloyd's student ID, 4 camisoles, and a pair of gray sweatpants

Although it was not revealed to the public, the police also seized photos and videos that depicted teenage girls engaged in sexual acts, which were downloaded from the internet onto Williams's home computer. It must be said that they found the same kind of pornography on his work computer located in his office on the military base. To this day, there is still speculation as to why this information was not disclosed. Could this have been an arrangement to protect Williams against fellow prisoners, or just to keep from publicly shaming him? Even more, could this arrangement have been made to protect the military?

What I also found quite interesting is that Williams's wife,

Mary Elizabeth, submitted a widely-reported claim against the Ontario Provincial Police for scratches to her hardwood floors, believed to have happened when the police dragged out the boxes of evidence. She had insisted that the police replace the section of floor that was damaged, not just repair it by sanding and coating it.

Police agreed to settle the claim by paying Harriman $3,000 for the damaged floor, as well as another $1,400 to replace a broken lamp also claimed to have been damaged by the police during their search. Police refused to discuss the payout of the claim, which really upset the public, as they felt that Williams himself should have been responsible for the damage rather than the taxpayers.

A week after his arrest, investigators reported that, along with hidden keepsakes and other evidence they had found in his home, they had matched a print from one of the homicide scenes to his boot.

In addition to the four primary incidents, the investigation into Williams included probes into 48 cases of theft of women's underwear dating back to 2006. In the searches of his Ottawa home, police discovered stolen lingerie that was neatly stored, cataloged, and concealed.

Even though Williams was placed on suicide watch at the Quinte Detention Centre in Napanee, Ontario, on April 2010, just one day before Easter Sunday, Williams jammed his cell door lock with cardboard and crumpled foil that he had saved from the juice cups that the prison served for breakfast every morning. He then put a cardboard toilet paper roll, also filled with the same cardboard and foil in it, down his throat.

When the staff heard the gagging noises being made by Williams, they managed to get into the jammed cell door and save his life. On his cell wall, there was a suicide note, written in mustard, which said that his affairs were in order now and that his feelings were too much to bear. After this, the guards used the nickname "Colonel Mustard" any time they talked about him.

TRIAL OF RUSSELL WILLIAMS

"A criminal trial is never about seeking justice for the victim. If it were, there could be only one verdict: Guilty." - Alan Dershowitz

Mary Elizabeth Harriman was noticeably missing from the hearing following her husband's arrest. She had taken a leave of absence from her job at the Heart and Stroke Foundation in Ottawa and gone into hiding.

There was also a silence among her coworkers, as they all refused to speak to the press about anything to do with the case. Williams's mother, who was working at the Sunnybrook Health Science Centre in Toronto, also had not spoken publicly and had avoided all media requests. However, Harvey Williams, Russell Williams's brother, also a family doctor who lived in Bowmanville, a suburb of Toronto, had issued a written statement to the media. He had explained that his brother Russell had been estranged from both him and his mother due to a rift that happened during the separation of their mother from their stepfather.

Harvey also explained that he and his mother had reached out to Russell just over two years earlier, but they had only maintained minimal contact since then. In fact, Harvey and their mother had shown up to Russell's command ceremony several months earlier, only to be seated in the second row, behind Williams's wife and his stepfather.

It was less than 24 hours after Williams had appeared in court when the base he had formally commanded had a parade for his replacement, Colonel David Cochrane, who had been promoted to the rank of Lieutenant Colonel. Cochrane promised to turn the page and soldier on, without looking back. It certainly would be a challenge that would put the base to the test.

On October 18, 2010, Williams pleaded guilty to all charges. On the first day of Williams's trial and guilty plea, details emerged of other sexual assaults he committed, including that of a new mother who was awakened by a blow to the head while she and her baby were asleep in her house. The first day of trial revealed that Williams also had pedophilic tendencies, stealing underwear of girls as young as nine years old. He made 82 fetish-related home invasions and attempted break-ins between September 2007 and November 2009.

Williams had progressed from break-ins to sexual assaults with no penetration to rape and murder. He had kept detailed track of police reports of the crimes he was committing, logged his crimes, kept photos and videos, and had even left notes and messages for his victims. In a break-in into the bedroom of a 12year-old girl, he left a message in her computer saying "Merci" ("thank you" in French).

He had taken thousands of pictures of his crimes and had kept the photos on his computer. Crown Attorney Robert Morrison presented numerous pictures of Williams dressed in the various pieces of underwear and bras he had stolen, frequently masturbating while lying on the beds of his victims.

Williams entered the courtroom wearing a dark gray suit and quietly pleaded,

> "Guilty, your honor."

Crown Attorney Lee Burgess then addressed the court,

> "In relation to each of the murders of Comeau and Lloyd, his crimes have been deliberate, both during committing the sexual assault and while confining the victims."

Jessica Lloyd's mother, Roxanne, was seated in the courtroom holding a large framed picture of her daughter. Also in the courtroom was Laurie Massicotte, Williams's second sexual assault victim, along with about 40 other victims and family members.

An agreed statement of facts was read out in court following a timeline of escalation in Williams's crimes. Crown prosecutor Robert Morrison drew attention to Williams's dangerous escalation of repeat break-ins. Morrison said,

> "Williams's repeated sexually obsessive behavior dates back to 2007 and 2008, long before he escalated to actual sexual assaults on women, or to the eventual murders of Comeau and Lloyd. In some of the photos, Williams is in girl's lingerie, wearing parts of his Canadian military uniform."

Many of the victims' family members had left the courtroom once Williams pleaded guilty. People in the public gallery were shedding tears and shaking their heads. Even seasoned reporters were showing signs of anxiety during the ongoing images that were being displayed.

Speaking to reporters outside the courtroom was Andy Lloyd, brother of Williams's second murder victim Jessica Lloyd.

> "I have plenty of friends with teenage daughters, and it's terrible. Nobody likes to hear something like that. Sitting here and hearing stuff that doesn't even involve my sister makes me angry as a Canadian, as a regular human being. It makes me angry."

Some of the photos presented on the first day of his trial were published in several newspapers. As some newspapers explained, although troubling, the photos were published because they capture the essence of the crimes of Williams and show the true nature of his crimes. Among the news media that published some of the released photographs were *The Montreal Gazette* and *The Toronto Star*.

On October 22, 2010, Ontario Superior Court Justice Robert F. Scott sentenced Williams to two concurrent terms of life in prison with no chance of parole for 25 years.

The Canadian Forces stripped Williams of his rank and medals and later dishonorably discharged him. At a news conference on the afternoon of the plea by Williams, the Department of Defense announced that it would strip Williams's rank, military decorations, and honors as quickly as possible. He will not be able to call himself a retired colonel and will simply be a civilian. Before his discharge, he was visited and examined by a military doctor in Kingston Penitentiary, as all outgoing military personnel must undergo a medical examination. Williams's uniform was burned and his medals were later cut into pieces, his commission scroll (a document confirming his status as a serving officer) was shredded, and his Pathfinder was crushed and scrapped.

Williams currently collects a $60,000 annual military pension.

In May 2010, he and his wife also split their real estate holdings, leaving Williams the sole owner of their cottage in Tweed and his wife the sole owner of their Ottawa townhouse.

Williams refused to pay $8,000 in victim surcharge fines, resulting in action being taken against him by a collection agency.

Williams was initially incarcerated at Kingston Penitentiary in the prison's segregation unit. After the prison began the process of closing, he was moved to a maximum security prison in Port-Cartier, Quebec on May 10, 2012.

WHO ARE THE PEOPLE IN YOUR NEIGHBORHOOD?

"I want you to be concerned about your next-door neighbor. Do you know your next-door neighbor?"
- Mother Teresa

Orleans, Ontario is known as a quiet family community outside of Canada's capital city of Ottawa, Ontario with a population of about 107,000. It's known for being the home of Elizabeth Manley, who became the 1988 Silver Medalist in Figure Skating at the Calgary Olympics, and is the home to many of the military and their families, as the National Defense Headquarters is located in Ottawa. Among the residents in Orleans were Russell Williams and his wife, Mary Elizabeth Harriman, who bought a corner lot home at 545 Wilkie Drive, a quiet street, and lived there for 13 years.

Most nights, there was a small gathering of neighbors on

Wilkie Drive, usually on the front patio of the Gagnes' house. Bob and Terry would welcome Shirley Fraser, George and Shirley White, as well as their newest neighbors, the Williamses. They would often have coffee and talk about local events and gossip.

Quite often they found themselves sitting and watching Russell go for his evening jog, and quite often would tease him. George White remembers Russell coming back from his run and saying to him "Where did you go today, Kanata?" Little did they know what Williams was up to while he was out on his jogs, where he was looking for new victims and gathering as much information as he could so that he could return to their residence and perform one of his many break-ins or even more.

Both Harriman and Williams would cross the street and spend time with their neighbors. Neither would drink coffee, but they would stand and talk. "She was much more talkative. She was more open than he was," remembers Terry Gagne.

> "He would look at you occasionally, but he almost always stared into the ground."

Neither Harriman nor Williams discussed much about their private lives during their visits. Shirley White remembers Harriman. "She would discuss her work, her cat, and golf, but always be very professional." The couple were also known for devoting a lot of time to their cat, Curio. They had no children and often treated Curio as their baby, leaving the blinds open when they were both away. Russ would even have the cat on his shoulder quite often when he came to visit the neighbors for coffee, remembers George Fraser, who fed the cat when they were both away.

Around their home in Orleans, Russ was always seen carrying Mary's luggage in the house for her and would always hold the doors open for her, and was considered very polite.

Harriman and Williams would spend long periods of time apart, as their jobs were very demanding and required them to do quite a large amount of traveling. In 2004, they purchased a $178,000 cottage located in Tweed, Ontario, just about a two-hour drive from their home in Orleans. It was a much smaller community of about 6,000 people in a mainly rural setting. This was to alleviate the three-hour commute for Russell five days a week in which he had to drive to the base to work every Monday through Friday.

Their Tweed neighbor, Larry Jones, says Harriman liked to read paperback novels in a lounge chair. Jones said he would have a glass of wine or beer with the couple occasionally, and said,

> "Russ was very polite and formal with his wife in public, always asking her if he could bring her a glass of wine or something. He would also always call her by both of her first names, Mary Elizabeth."

One thing Jones also remembered was that Mary would be in Ottawa most of the time, as she worked there, but the Colonel would be in Tweed most of the time alone.

> "He was kind of a loner because he never really had any friends there to speak of; maybe twice a year he'd have some friends there."

One of Williams's visitors at their Cosy Cove Lane cottage in Tweed was Jeff Farquhar, his longtime friend since 1982 when they were roommates in college. "I remember being there when he had first bought it. I think the deal was just barely done and he called me to come out and look, and then gave me a tour," Jeff said.

Both seemed to be enjoying successful careers and continued to advance. Harriman was promoted to senior executive for the Heart and Stroke Foundation of Canada. Russell was advanced to commander of CFB Trenton, the country's largest Air Force Base. Shirley Fraser remembers some of the neighbors who had been invited to Russell's promotion ceremony. "Mary Elizabeth seemed thrilled to pieces when the boys had agreed to go down and attend her husband being promoted up in the ranks."

So just a few months later, many on Wilkie Street were surprised when a "For Sale" sign went up in the couple's front yard. It seemed that neither Harriman or Williams had told any of them about their plans. "We were quite shocked when we saw the sign go up," says White. "We thought, oh, no, they were such great neighbors. What will happen? Who will move in?"

The couple had bought a new high-end townhome in a trendy part of town, on Edison Avenue in Ottawa. Soon afterward, they said their goodbyes to their neighbors of 13 years and moved.

Less than two months later, news of Williams's arrest hit the Wilkie Street neighborhood. "A few of us close friends went through three stages," says White. "The first stage when the blast of the news came out, we said, can't be, can't be, they've made a mistake, it can't be our Russ."

Then, as more details emerged, the group began to think that Williams was guilty, even though they still didn't believe it. White said,

> "Yes, he's guilty. We feel we've been betrayed by the friendship, but anyway, life goes on."

George White, a retired Air Force technician, wrote letters to both Williams and Harriman after the news broke about Williams's arrest. To Williams, he wrote expressing his regret that the Colonel's life had gone so wrong. To Harriman, he wrote that he supported her unconditionally. But neither of them has written back to him.

Shirley Fraser believes that Harriman was victimized by her husband.

> "My biggest prayer is that she will be able to get through this. I can't imagine what she's going through."

Harriman was not in Belleville to be with her husband during his interrogation. In fact, ever since her husband's arrest, she has completely avoided the public spotlight that came with the case. Yet she remains the focus of several lawsuits, being accused of knowing about Williams's sexual assaults and other criminal behavior.

Both court documents and Williams's own recorded confession suggest that

Harriman had no idea of her husband's secret life and, in fact, really believed that Russell was a very good person with a fine moral compass. Harriman wrote in the civil suit affidavit

> "On or about February 8, 2010, I became aware of criminal charges against my husband. The revelation of these charges has been devastating to me."

To date, this is all we have heard from her, as she still refuses to speak to any media about her husband.

But there was one neighbor who wasn't so worried about what Williams was going to face in jail. Larry Jones,

Williams's Tweed neighbor, had been affected like no other neighbor, as he was a victim as well.

When Williams was arrested, Jones's phone was ringing off the hook from people around the country, either to congratulate him or sympathize with him. In fact, Jones's email inbox was so full that he gave up even trying to answer them.

Jones knew Williams had tried to set him up as the fall guy in his crimes, and it was still one thing that was bothering him. It seemed far too convenient that Russell had placed the body of Jessica Lloyd on the side of the road at the camp where Jones would go hunting. He recalled the conversation that he had with Williams on a previous September day. That day, Jones had been dressed in his camouflage gear and loading up his truck with a crossbow and rifle to go hunting. Williams walked over and said, "What's happening today?"

"Oh, I'm just going partridge hunting," Jones responded.

"So you hunt, do you? There's partridge around here?" the Colonel asked. Jones thought that was strange, as he was sure Williams knew he went hunting a lot and that there were plenty of partridge around the area, but he put it down to an awkward conversation between a city slicker and a country boy.

"There's plenty of partridge out at the camp on East Hungerford Road," Jones told him.

"East Hungerford Road...doesn't ring a bell," Williams replied.

"It's out by the golf course, you go up there past Cary Road, and our camp is right there," Jones answered him.

"Oh, really? That's good. Well, good luck with the hunting, and we'll see you later," Williams said as he started to walk back to his cottage.

Equally as suspicious, the day before Jessica Lloyd went missing, Larry had come home to find his workshop unlocked even though he remembered locking it the night before. He quickly looked around inside the shop. He was worried about all the expensive power tools and equipment that he had stored and bought for his workshop. As he went through everything, he soon realized that nothing major was missing. In fact, the only things gone were an old jacket that was used for the dog to sleep on, a pair of gloves, and his lighter. Who would take the trouble to break into his workshop and take nothing but old used clothing?

Jones now believes that the clothes were stolen either by Williams or by one of the police who had suspected him in the spree of violent crimes. This was the beginning of the nightmare for Larry Jones.

Jones returned home from a partridge hunting trip in October of 2009 to find dozens of police officers going through his home. He was taken in for questioning, and per his statement in a later lawsuit that was filed against the police, officers also interrogated his wife of 40 years, asking whether Larry participated in bondage.

He was told that the investigation was related to the break-ins and sexual assaults that were happening around Tweed.

But word quickly spread throughout the neighborhood that Jones was a suspect in the case.

One of the sexual assault victims, Laurie Massicotte, told police she couldn't identify her attacker because she had been blindfolded, but thought she might have heard his voice before. She then led the police to believe that the attacker could have been Jones. Massicotte also told police that the attacker was not a tall or big person and was between 30 to 40 years old, but Jones was 65 at the time, stood 5' 9", and weighed 215 pounds.

Fifteen years earlier, Jones's son, Greg, had worked at Sears with co-worker Warren Lloyd, who just happened to be Jessica Lloyd's father. Warren was having problems with his water pump and asked Greg for help with it. Greg had called his father and asked him to go over and see if he could fix the pump. Larry drove over to Lloyd's house and fixed the pump without charge. This happened to be the same house where Jessica would later get raped and beaten, so Larry also knew that his prints were going to be all over that house.

Even when Jones tried to report the break-in of his workshop, OPP detective Russ Alexander replied, "What do you want me to do about it?" For some reason, Alexander was not letting go of the idea that Jones committed the crimes. In fact, even the day that Williams was being charged and had confessed, Alexander was interviewing witnesses about Jones and the murder of Jessica Lloyd.

Even when Jones's wife, Bonnie, tried to get their belongings that had been seized by the police three months later, she was advised by Detective Alexander that the police were continuing to investigate Larry for the attacks, per the lawsuit documents.

The lawsuit by Jones and his wife was eventually dropped on October 13, 2013. Even though there are still people who no longer speak to him or that look at him in a negative way, Jones looks at it as a valuable learning lesson.

But there was still one thing that had stayed in the back of Jones's mind, about his own granddaughters. When all the attacks were happening and they would take the bus out to see their grandfather, and Jones was still out hunting, they would take the bus to Williams's house and wait there for him, as it was considered the safest place for them to wait.

13

WHEN ALL IS SAID, AND DONE

"Life is really simple, but we seem to want to make it complicated." - Confucius

Mary Elizabeth Harriman's future once seemed perfectly secure. She and her husband both pulled in six-figure salaries. Their careers were in ascendance. That financial security, however, is now as uncertain as so many of the things that Harriman once took for granted.

The first two multi-million dollar lawsuits were not only against the convicted murderer, Russell Williams, but his wife as well, and were filed just four years after his conviction.

Williams's first sexual assault victim, whose name is still withheld from the public, was suing for $2.45 million, and Jessica Lloyd's mother and brother were suing for $4 million. Not only were both parties suing Williams for his brutal and vicious attacks on the victims, but they accused his wife of participating in a fraudulent property transfer to hide their assets from any lawsuits. Harriman had paid her husband $62,000 in cash and assumed the remaining mortgage on their newly built $700,000 Ottawa home. These lawsuits were settled out of court for an undisclosed amount, by Williams himself, and they dismissed the suit against his wife. Despite these settlements, Williams's legal battles were far from over.

Up next was the lawsuit by his second sexual assault victim, Laurie Massicotte. Her claim was for $7 million, and again it was against both Russell and his wife, Mary Elizabeth Harriman. Massicotte was also alleging Harriman was aware of her husband's home invasions and sexual assaults. She also accused the Ontario Provincial Police of failing to warn the community about the predator.

Harriman denied any wrongdoing and answered the lawsuit in a court filing, saying, "I had absolutely no intention of shielding assets, and the property deal was initiated to ensure my financial security." She also stated, "I was devastated to learn the truth about my husband. I, too, am a victim."

Harriman's lawyer, Mary Jane Binks, said that the lawsuit was settled in November of 2016. Binks said,

> "The civil action launched by Laurie Massicotte has now been settled. All parties want their privacy."

Details of the settlement were not disclosed. Massicotte chose to reveal her identity and speak publicly about her ordeal. In her statement of claim, Massicotte said she had been bound and sexually assaulted by Williams in her home in September 2009. She said in the claim that the attack against her left her fearful, humiliated, depressed, suicidal, and unable to function in society. It also said she would require extensive therapy.

The Tweed cottage, purchased for $178,000, was transferred to Williams. In 2013, the cottage was sold by Williams to his one-time neighbors and first victims, the Murdochs. They were living right next door to the Colonel and probably sleeping when Williams brought home victim Jessica Lloyd and killed her, right in that same cottage. Per their interview with *Macleans* magazine, their motivation was to help the primary victims out by purchasing the property, as the money would go to help settle the outstanding lawsuits.

They also wanted to revitalize the property which had been a long abandoned eyesore. More than anything, they wanted to ensure Lloyd's devastated family would receive the dignity they deserve. "We'll never be able to forget what happened there, even if we rebuild another house on that lot," says Ron. "It's part of the history of that lot. We'll never be able to forget that, and we shouldn't. She lost her life there. But respect will always be given. There will be no cameras in there. There will be no big splash."

You might be asking why the victims and victims' families were so set on holding Harriman responsible for her husband's crime. There are many things to consider. How it is that Harriman never saw any of the hundreds of pairs of women's panties, bras, dresses, and other various pieces of clothing, just lying about the house, in open, unconcealed places, such as the laundry room? How did she not see any of the pictures or films, not only left in many of the bags that were sitting around the house, but also on the Mac computer that she had shared with Williams? On that computer, Williams had put many of the pictures and films of his assaults, home invasions, and even ones of the dead victims, all in organized files, where it was easy to access the victim, date, and type of crime with one click.

Per a *Macleans* magazine interview, Laurie Massicotte believed that Mary Elizabeth was aware of her husband's illicit conduct but did not report the crimes to the police. Massicotte also claimed that Williams's longtime spouse "gained financially from this illicit conduct by acquiring Williams's assets after he was captured, including half of the couple's Ottawa home."

Both Laurie Massicotte and Jessica Lloyd's families lawsuits were not only against Russell Williams and his long-time wife, Mary Elizabeth Harriman, but also against the Ontario Provincial Police. You see, when Williams assaulted the unnamed victim in mid-September 2009, he left some DNA on her neck. That evidence was processed and uploaded into the RCMP DNA databank within two weeks. Later that year, on November 24, Williams attacked and killed Marie-France Comeau. Again DNA was taken at the crime scene, but this time it took 10 weeks for the police to process and upload it into the same RCMP DNA data bank.

During that 10 weeks, Williams had killed again — he tortured, raped, and then killed Jessica Lloyd. The 10-week time was way over the 30-day target that was suggested by Justice Archie Campbell. A quicker upload would have linked the Comeau murder with the sexual assault in Tweed. Would that have led the police to investigating the military man or somebody who was in the living proximity of both victims? I don't think that we could possibly know the answer to that, but it would have significantly advanced the investigation for sure. Andy Lloyd, Jessica's brother, at the time made the statement,

> "It doesn't make sense that DNA results aren't available much faster."

Another strange coincidence that happened with the police was on the night of Jessica Lloyd's murder. While Williams was sitting in his truck, parked in the vacant lot beside her house waiting for Lloyd to come home, a Belleville police officer spotted his truck. He considered it suspicious and stopped at Jessica's home and knocked on her door. When he received no answer, he left. It was just a few hours later that Jessica arrived home and was assaulted and killed.

EPILOGUE

The One Little Goat theatre company out of Toronto has decided to start running a show this March of 2017 called *Smyth/Williams*. The play is based on the intense interrogation in which Williams ended up confessing to his crimes to then Detective Smyth, per the *Calgary Herald* report on January 23, 2017.

Adam Seelig, the director of the theatre company said,

> "I first got the idea for the play in 2010, when Williams's case and confession to Detective Smyth was making all the headlines."

Seelig was amazed at the time by Smyth's ingenuity and chilled by Williams's 'matter-of-fact' manner of confession.

The play will have an all-female group performing as a direct link to the recent urgency of violence against women, especially against women in the military.

ACKNOWLEDGMENTS

Thank you to my editor, proofreaders, and to the cover artist for your support! Also, I must thank my family at home as well as my family on the radio, you take me up!

I want to thank the editor, proofreaders and all support staff for helping me with this project: Book Cover Design: Kat @ Evening Sky Publishing Services; Proofreaders: Bettye McKee, Robyn MacEachern, Kathi Garcia, Ron Steed, Sandra Miller and Selene MacLeod

ABOUT THE AUTHOR

Alan R Warren has written several Best-Selling True Crime books and has been one of the hosts and producer of the popular NBC news talk radio show 'House of Mystery' which reviews True Crime, History, Science, Religion,
Paranormal Mysteries that we live with every day from a darker, comedic and logical perspective and has interviewed guests such as Robert Kennedy Jr., F. Lee Bailey, Aphrodite Jones, Marcia Clark, Nancy Grace, Dan Abrams and Jesse Ventura. The show is based in Seattle on KKNW 1150 A.M. and syndicated on the NBC network throughout the United States including on KCAA 106.5 F.M. Los Angeles/Riverside/Palm Springs, as well in Utah, New Mexico, and Arizona.

ALSO BY ALAN R. WARREN

DOOMSDAY CULTS: THE DEVIL'S HOSTAGES

Jim Jones convinced his 1000 followers they would all have to commit suicide since he was going to die. Shoko Asahara convinced his followers to release a weapon of mass destruction, the deadly sarin gas, on a Tokyo subway. The Order of the Solar Temple lured the rich and famous, including Princess Grace of Monaco, and convinced them to die a fiery death now on Earth to be reborn on a better planet called Sirius. Charles Manson convinced his followers to kill, in an attempt to incite an apocalyptic race war.

These are a few of the doomsday cults examined in this book by bestselling author Alan R. Warren. Its focus is on cults whose destructive behavior was due in large part to their apocalyptic beliefs or doomsday movements. It includes details surrounding the massacres and a look into how their members became so brainwashed they committed unimaginable crimes at the command of their leader.

Usually, when we hear about these cults and their massacres, we ask ourselves how it possibly happened. We could also ask ourselves, what then is the difference between a cult and a religion? We once had a small group of people who unquestionably followed a person who believed he was the son of God. Two thousand years later, that following is one of the most recognized religions in the world. This book in no way criticizes believing in God. Rather, it examines how a social movement grows into a full religion and when it does not. And what makes the conventional faiths such as Christianity, Judaism, Islam, and Hinduism stand above groups such as the Branch Davidians or Children of God.

IN CHAINS: THE DANGEROUS WORLD OF HUMAN TRAFFICKING

Human trafficking is the trade of people for forced labor or sex. It also includes the illegal extraction of human organs and tissues. And it is an extremely ruthless and dangerous industry plaguing our world today.

Most believe human trafficking occurs in countries with no human rights legislation. This is a myth. All types of human trafficking are alive and well in most of the developed countries of the world like the United States, Canada, and the UK. It is estimated that $150 billion a year is generated in the forced labor industry alone. It is also believed that 21 million people are trapped in modern day slavery – exploited for sex, labor, or organs.

Most also believe since they live in a free country, there is built-in protection against such illegal practices. But for many, this is not the case. Traffickers tend to focus on the most vulnerable in our society, but trafficking can happen to anyone. You will see how easy it can happen in the stories included in *In Chains*.

REFERENCES AND SOURCES

1. Emerson, Dianne: *Psychopaths in our Lives: My Interviews*, Oct. 5, 2016, ISBN-10: 1-517307880, ISBN-13: 978-15170377882, plus a two-hour interview by phone with her about the possible condition of Russel Williams and his family.
2. Appleby, Timothy: *A New Kind of Monster: The Secret Life and Chilling Crimes of Colonel Russell Williams*, August 23, 2011, ISBN-10: 0307359514, ISBN-13:978-0307359513.
3. CBC Fifth Estate: Sept. 24, 2010 Season 36 Episode 1.
4. CBC Fifth Estate: Oct. 22, 2010 Season 36 Episode 5.
5. Pollanen, DR.: Postmortem Exam - Cause of Death, Corporal Marie-France Comeau.
6. Police Transcripts of the videos taken by Russell Williams. The tapes have only been seen by police, crown prosecutors and defence - cannot be independently evaluated.

7. The Star: *Woman Settles Lawsuit Against Sex Killer Russell Williams and his Wife,* Canadian Press, Oct 12, 2016.
8. Mehta, Diana: *Ontario Woman's Lawsuit Against Russell Williams Settled,* Globe and Mail, Oct. 12, 2016.
9. Rankin, Jim and Contenta, Sandro: *The Secret Life of Colonel Russell Williams Exposed,* Toronto Star, Oct.18, 2010.
10. Friscolanti. Michael: *Serial Killer Russell Williams Has Sold Infamous Cottage,* Macleans, May 22, 2013.
11. Seglins, Steve: *Russell Williams's neighbor Sues After Suspected in Crimes,* CBC News, Nov. 28, 2011.
12. Hendry, Luke: *Lawsuit Against Russell Williams Dropped,* Toronto Sun, Oct. 16, 2013.
13. Gibb, David A.: *Camouflaged Killer: The Shocking Double Life of Canadian Air Force Colonel Russell Williams,* Oct. 4, 2011, Berkely ISBN-10: 0425244393 ISBN-13:978-0425244395.
14. Vronsky, Peter; *Serial Killers: The Method and Madness of Monsters,* Oct. 5, 2004, ISBN-10:0425196402 ISBN-13:978-0425196403.
15. Ottawa Edition: *Accused Killer Colonel Russell Williams and Paul Bernardo,* QMI Agency, Feb. 12, 2010.
16. Tripp, Rob: *Accused Sex Killer Colonel Russell Williams Attempts Jailhouse Suicide,* Globe and Mail, Apr. 4, 2010.

17. CBC News: *Colonel Russell Williams Pleads Guilty to all 88 Charges*, Oct. 18, 2010.
18. 2010 Trial Transcripts, Crown v. Williams 2009, *Interrogation of Williams by OPP*.
19. Live Radio Interview with Laurie Massicotte.

www.ingramcontent.com/pod-product-compliance
Lightning Source LLC
Chambersburg PA
CBHW062208100526
44589CB00014B/2010